Sweet Things

Sweet Things

chocolates,
candies,
caramels &
marshmallows—
to make & give

Annie Rigg

Photography
by Tara Fisher

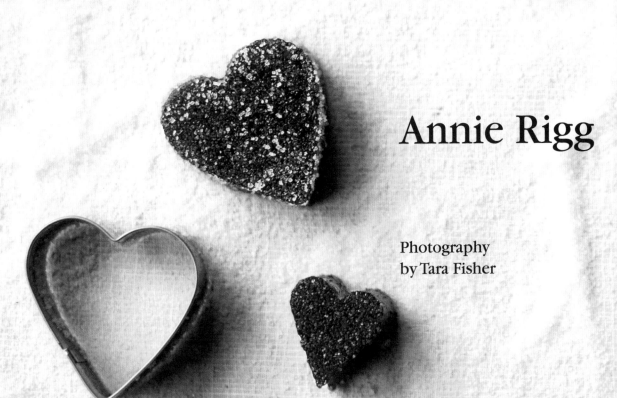

Kyle Books

To H.D.
Sweets for My Sweet
x

Published in 2014 by Kyle Books
www.kylebooks.com
general.enquiries@kylebooks.com

Distributed by National Book Network
4501 Forbes Blvd., Suite 200
Lanham, MD 20706
Phone: (800) 462-6420
Fax: (800) 338-4550
customercare@nbnbooks.com

First published in Great Britain in 2013 by Kyle Books,
an imprint of Kyle Cathie Ltd.

10 9 8 7 6 5 4 3 2 1

ISBN 978-1-909487-15-4

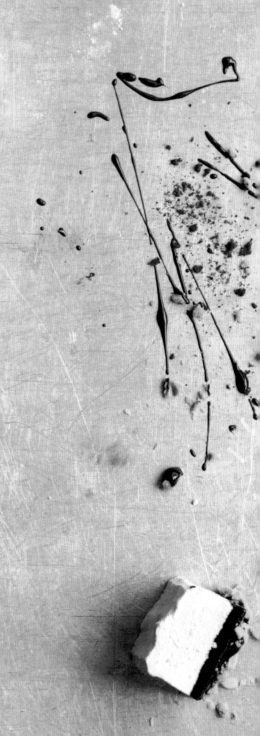

Text © 2013 Annie Rigg
Design © 2013 Kyle Books
Photographs © 2013 Tara Fisher
Annie Rigg is hereby identified as the author of this work in
accordance with Section 77 of the Copyright, Designs and
Patents Act 1988.

Editor: Judith Hannam
Editorial Assistant: Tara O'Sullivan
Copy Editor: Anne Newman
Designer: Lucy Gowans
Photographer: Tara Fisher
Food Stylist: Annie Rigg
Prop Stylist: Tabitha Hawkins
Production: Nic Jones and David Hearn

Library of Congress Control Number: 2014939209

Color reproduction by ALTA London
Printed and bound in China by C & C Offset Printing Co., Ltd.

Contents

There's no denying it— I have a sweet tooth.

I always have and imagine that I always will. I am drawn like a moth to a flame when it comes to eating or cooking sweet things and I feel an almost gravitational pull toward candy shops and chocolatiers. Shelves of glass jars filled with candies all the colors of the rainbow and every flavor imaginable, trays of cocoa-dusted truffles and brightly colored foil-wrapped chocolate bars, intoxicating to the eye as well as the taste buds—I am in heaven when surrounded by such delights.

My earliest and fondest food memories all involve things that are sugar-loaded—as a small child, I vividly remember small pink-and-white striped paper bags filled with alphabet candies in pale pastel colors, sharing a caramel-filled chocolate bar with my mother after swimming lessons, and toffees with my grandfather while on country walks.

We were given pocket money for the weekend to spend on whatever treats we liked—this was only a matter of a few pennies and it required careful consideration as to how it could be most wisely spent. It was an early lesson in candy economics. Was my pocket money best spent on a mixed bag of one-penny sweets or a few ounces of tangy sweet-tarts, gumdrops, or lollipops? These choices taught me to refine my candy tastes from an early age.

This passion for all things sweet has now translated into my kitchen and cooking. Candy making is not dissimilar to baking (which incidentally shares an equal billing in my life) in that it requires a little quiet kitchen time, with few interruptions or disturbances, and results in the kind of food that gives joy both to yourself and the lucky folks who share your endeavors. An hour or so dedicated to the wonders of marshmallow or nougat making is, in my opinion, time well spent. You will find yourself popular among friends and family who will love you all the more when they are presented with the fruits of your labors because, after all, homemade candies are for giving and sharing. Candies are most certainly not an essential food group, they are not one of your five-a-day (far from it!) but they do make life more delicious.

There is a sweet treat for just about every occasion—whether it's Christmas, Valentine's Day, Easter, weddings, or wedding showers. Traditional red- and white-striped candy canes adorning the festive table, heart-shaped marshmallows or chocolate truffles for your loved ones, and Candy Buttons or Candy with Lollipop Dippers for kids' parties—let no occasion go unnoticed as far as homemade candies are concerned.

Not only do I love making candies, I love giving them, too. Something delicious and beautifully packaged that says, "I thought about you, what you'd like most and would make you smile." Giving a ribbon-tied box of homemade truffles as a "thank you" for dinner would be so much more appreciated than a store-bought box of chocolates. I imagine that most of the recipes in this book are likely to be made as gifts or for an occasion, but that doesn't mean that there's anything stopping you from making Hazelnut Caramel Nougat for fun, Salted Butterscotch Popcorn for movie night, or Fruit Roll-ups for kids' lunchboxes or simply because you feel in the mood.

All of the recipes in this book have been thoroughly tested in a domestic kitchen using regular equipment, and require nothing more fancy than a sugar thermometer, a couple of good-quality, heavy-bottomed pans, and perhaps a few chocolate or candy molds. I have tried to use equipment such as pans in sizes that you may already have in your kitchen or are easily sourced or substituted. Good-quality chocolate and candy molds are now available to the home cook; they were once the preserve of professional candy makers and chocolatiers but a quick search on the internet shows up molds in every conceivable shape, size, and budget. It's never been easier to make your own chocolates or sweets.

I am all too aware of the pitfalls of candy making at home. Most of my early attempts were disasters due to lack of preparation—trying to prepare a pan, juggle a thermometer and a saucepan of scalding hot syrup, chop some almonds, and hastily melt chocolate in the microwave (most likely burning it) all at the same time is bound to end in chaos. If a recipe says to chop the nuts and melt the chocolate in the first paragraph, the instruction is there for a reason and it probably means that I have, at some stage, burned nuts, spilled melted chocolate on the floor, covered the kitchen in molten caramel and the dog in marshmallow, and had to start all over again.

Preparation is key to success in all candy making—have your ingredients measured and prepared and your pans lined before you even consider starting to melt any chocolate or boil any syrup.

Never underestimate the formidable and sneaky powers of a pan of boiling syrup—it can sometimes seem like it has a mind of its own. It will know when you're about to do a load of laundry, send an email, or answer the phone. You can be watching the pan like a hawk, the temperature creeping painfully slowly upward, but the moment that your back is turned it will shoot over and above the point that you wanted and you will have to start again. Any recipe involving boiling syrup is best taken at a steady pace rather than tackled like a bull in a china shop—scalding hot sugar, haste, and carelessness are a dangerous combination, so give yourself plenty of time and space.

I have tried, where possible, to keep the recipe quantities to a sensible amount to make things easy for the home cook—there is nothing more unnerving than wrestling a vast pan of boiling hot, molten fudge or attempting to temper an enormous bowlful of expensive chocolate. Most of the candies in this book will have a shorter shelf life than their store-bought cousins, but if properly packaged, most will keep for at least a week. I have never found that homemade candies sit around for too long anyway—the opposite is mostly true—as soon as they are made, they disappear in a flash and often before they can even be packaged.

There is a candy for every season, occasion, and level of culinary skill, and much satisfaction to be found for the sweet-toothed, candy-loving cook. So arm yourself with a sugar thermometer, seek out some fabulous-tasting chocolate, and discover the joy of making homemade candies for yourself.

Basics

Sugar Thermometers

Some people (my mother included) have an irrational fear of any recipe that requires the use of a sugar thermometer. This I don't understand. Why waste time, effort, and ingredients on guesswork? A sugar thermometer is your friend, your insurance policy, and in my kitchen, a workhorse. Thermometers are not expensive and will cost you roughly the same amount as the ingredients needed for two failed attempts at making fudge or caramel as a result of not using one. You wouldn't set out to make a cake and guess the weight of the ingredients and the oven temperature; the same goes for thermometers and candy making. All of the recipes in this book that suggest the use of a sugar thermometer have been written and tested using one, and for perfect results I suggest that you use one, too.

I prefer to use an old-fashioned brass thermometer that has either Celsius or Fahrenheit measurements in an easy-to-read scale—this makes checking temperatures very quick at a glance—and has the added bonus that it can be washed in hot soapy water. With this type of thermometer I don't have to worry about flat batteries or damaged digital parts. However, no matter what type you use, it is wise to calibrate your thermometer before use, to double-check that it is reading correctly, especially if it is new or hasn't been used for a while. Fear not—this is very easily done. Simply pop a pan of water on to the stove, stick the thermometer into the water, and bring to a boil. Once the water is boiling, the temperature should read 212°F—if it's a couple of degrees out then you will need to adjust the cooking temperatures of whatever candies you are making accordingly. If it's way off, I would suggest that you purchase a new one. I regularly calibrate my thermometer regardless of its age—every 4th or 5th time I use it—just to be certain of perfect readings every time.

Chocolate Tempering Thermometers

Unless you are an experienced chocolatier, you will find it hard to temper chocolate properly without the use of a chocolate thermometer. If you already have a digital-probe type sugar thermometer you will be able to use that for chocolate, too, but if not you'll need another especially for this purpose. Look for rubber spatulas that cleverly have a thermometer in the spoon part; this makes it easy to take accurate temperature readings from the chocolate itself rather than from the base of the bowl, which will be hotter. Thermometers that rest on the bottom of the bowl will give a hotter reading due to this. Make sure that your thermometer is spotlessly clean and dry before and after use—any unseen drops of water or grease will ruin the chocolate that you are tempering.

Ingredients

My mantra for all cooking is to use the best-quality ingredients that your budget allows for. And candy making is no exception to this rule.

I keep a variety of **sugars** in my pantry and always have a supply of superfine and brown sugars. Store sugar in airtight jars or boxes to prevent it from drying out or being tainted by other strong flavors. Brown sugar is especially susceptible to drying out if not kept airtight. Keep a supply of corn syrup, molasses, and condensed milk in your pantry, so that you can whip up a batch of fudge or caramel at a moment's notice.

Butter should always be fresh, good quality, and unsalted. Milk and cream should likewise be fresh and preferably, but not crucially, organic. The same applies to eggs, which should be at room temperature before use.

When buying **vanilla pods**, I tend to buy 10 or 15 vacuum-packed superior-quality pods from a specialist online supplier rather than buying them individually from the supermarket. Not only is this cheaper in the long run, but the vanilla comes in a variety of top grades and from a variety of sources from Uganda to Polynesia. Stored in an airtight jar or box, vanilla pods will last for months. Good-quality vanilla extract is now widely available and should never be confused with vanilla flavoring, which is quite a different beast and not one that I ever use in my kitchen. A good compromise is vanilla bean paste, which is a thick syrup containing a good dose of vanilla seeds and extract.

Now let's have a quick chat about **chocolate**. I use a large amount of chocolate in my cooking—not only in candy making but in baking, too—and I never skimp on quality. It is worth every penny to spend a little extra to buy the absolute best chocolate that you can afford. When using dark chocolate I like one with a cocoa content of around 60–68 percent; I find that this gives a perfect balance of flavor and richness. Anything higher than this can fight with the other ingredients that you are using and overpower more subtle flavors. But it's all about personal choice. Superior-quality chocolate, such as Valrhona, can be bought as chocolate chips rather than in large blocks—this makes melting easier. See page 172 for suppliers.

When using **fruit**, it should always be fresh and seasonal for best possible flavor. Dried fruit and nuts should also be well within their use-by dates—nuts that are past their best can become rancid and oily.

When using **salt** in a recipe I always use sea salt flakes (such as Maldon). This gives a superior, clean, salty flavor to all cooking.

I recommend using **sunflower oil** for greasing pans and equipment as it is flavorless, rather than vegetable oil, which can have a distinctly "savory" tang.

Weights and Measures

All spoon measurements in this book are level unless otherwise stated and I always—and I do mean always, without fail—use **measuring spoons**. Along with a good thermometer, these are some of the most used tools in my kitchen. If you're serious about cooking and don't already have some, please make the small investment. Teaspoons for stirring your tea or coffee come in all manner of shapes and sizes and will not give consistent results either in candy making or baking.

Digital scales are a must for accuracy. Some scales have the option to reset the weight to zero after adding each ingredient. This is incredibly useful and will make weighing multiple ingredients easier and quicker and cut down on washing. Simply put the saucepan or bowl on the scale, make sure the setting

is at zero, and add one ingredient at a time, re-setting to zero after each addition—this is especially useful when adding syrups or liquid glucose to sugar.

Other Equipment

A couple of **offset spatulas** in different sizes are immensely useful, and in particular a small one with an offset blade. This will make it a cinch to smooth the surface of marshmallows, nougat, or fudge when pouring mixtures into pans, or lifting small items such as truffles from pans or baking sheets.

Heatproof rubber spatulas are highly prized in my kitchen—I have a selection in different sizes and colors. They are ideal for stirring caramels, puree, and Turkish Delight and get into the corners of a pan where no wooden spoon would dare to venture.

Dipping forks for coating truffles in melted chocolate make light work of this sometimes messy task. They are inexpensive and come in a number of shapes and sizes. I use a round ball-shaped dipper for round truffles and a long three-pronged fork for square or rectangular shaped chocolates. Though not essential, they will make life easier than using a dinner fork for the same purpose.

Saucepans. I don't have a vast collection of pans in every size imaginable but the ones that I do have are heavy-bottomed, good quality, and will last for years to come. Solid bottoms on pans are essential for even cooking and to prevent sugar catching unevenly on the bottom of the pan. The three pans that I use most for sweet making have capacities of 1 quart, 1.8 quarts, and 2.5 quarts, and I find that these serve most of my candy-making needs. I also prefer to use saucepans that have one long handle rather than two side handles, as this makes steady pouring of boiling hot mixtures easier and safer.

Chocolate

Praline Hearts

Aztec Truffles

Earl Grey Tea Truffles

Peanut and Raspberry Truffle Pops

Sea-salted Caramel Truffles

Passion Fruit and Pistachio Truffles

Rose Truffles

Bitter Orange Chocolate Truffles

Chocolate Salami

Caramel Nougat Bars

Flødeboller

Peanut Butter Cups

Cherry Coconut Bombs

Chocolate Nougat Chunks

Almond Butterscotch Chocolate Crunch

Valentine Hearts

Peppermint Creams

Marzipan and Orange Chocolates

Speckled Mini Easter Eggs

Chocolate Bark

Dazzle Drops

Chocolate Bars

Hot Chocolate Dunkers

*M*ilk, white or dark, chocolate features heavily in my life—and in my kitchen. I can't imagine a day without tasting at least a morsel.

All of the chocolate recipes in this book were tested (and tasted) using high-quality chocolate such as Valrhona. There's a big world of chocolate to choose from, so take the time to seek out and try varieties from different countries and made from different beans to find what suits your taste, needs, and budget. When using dark chocolate, I prefer to use one with a medium-high cocoa content—somewhere around the 60–68 percent mark. Anything higher than this can overpower delicate flavors in your truffles and bars. Chocolate with a lower percentage might be a little on the sweet side; however, a higher cocoa percentage is not necessarily an indication of a superior-tasting or higher-quality chocolate—it simply means that the chocolate contains less sugar.

High-quality chocolate is now easily available either from specialist online suppliers or in gourmet food shops. Most quality brands are available in blocks or as chips (sometimes called pistoles or callets). I like chips because they are easy to use, measure, and melt. All chocolate should be well packed and stored in a cool, dry and dark place away from strongly flavored foods to avoiding becoming tainted.

In this chapter you will find recipes ranging from the simplest chocolate bark to melt-in-the-mouth truffles in an array of flavors to homemade chocolate bars and Easter eggs. There's something for every taste and skill here.

To temper or not to temper? This is entirely up to you, though remember that chocolate that hasn't been tempered won't have that sheen and snap that gives homemade chocolates a professional look. You can find instructions for chocolate tempering on page 24. Whatever you decide, your chocolate creations will still taste delicious.

I like heart shapes and so for these truffles I set the praline ganache into a shallow pan and stamped out heart shapes in assorted sizes before coating in either milk or dark chocolate. If you had plastic or silicone heart-shaped molds, you could use those—follow the instructions for creating a chocolate shell on page 51 for the Easter eggs and then fill with the ganache. Or if you have no inclination to make heart shapes, simply chill the ganache and roll into balls following the instructions for making truffles on page 16.

Praline *Hearts*

Makes 20–25

¾ cup blanched hazelnuts
⅓ cup superfine sugar
3oz dark chocolate
  (64 percent cocoa solids),
  chopped
5oz milk chocolate,
  chopped
½ cup heavy cream
½ teaspoon vanilla bean
  paste
pinch of salt

To coat
5oz milk chocolate,
  chopped
5oz dark chocolate,
  chopped
1 tablespoon crystallized
  roses or sugar sprinkles

Equipment
8 x 12-inch baking pan
heart-shaped cutters in
  assorted sizes
disposable piping bag

Store
Praline hearts will keep in the fridge for up to 1 week in an airtight box between sheets of parchment paper or waxed paper.

Preheat the oven to 325°F and line the baking sheet with nonstick parchment paper.

Toast the hazelnuts in the oven for 4 minutes until pale golden. Set aside.

Place the superfine sugar in a small, heavy-bottomed saucepan with 1 tablespoon water. Melt the sugar over low heat without stirring and use a clean pastry brush dipped in hot water to dissolve any sugar crystals that form on the sides of the pan. Once the sugar has dissolved bring the syrup to a boil and cook steadily until it becomes an amber-colored caramel. Add the hazelnuts to the pan, stir to combine, and then turn out onto a sheet of nonstick parchment paper. Leave to cool completely.

Break the praline into chunks, chop in a food processor until finely ground, and then continue to blend until you have a slightly granular paste, almost like peanut butter. Set aside while you prepare the ganache.

Place the dark and milk chocolate in a heatproof bowl with the heavy cream, vanilla, and salt and set it over a pan of barely simmering water, making sure the bottom of the bowl doesn't touch the water. Stir frequently until the chocolate has melted into the cream and the ganache is silky smooth. Remove from the pan and cool for a few minutes before folding in the hazelnut paste. Spoon the ganache into the prepared pan and spread level with an offset spatula. Leave to cool and then cover and chill until firm.

Turn the set ganache out of the pan and peel off the lining paper. Using the heart cutters, stamp out truffles in a variety of sizes and arrange on a clean sheet of parchment paper. Chill again while you prepare the chocolate for the coating.

Follow the instructions for tempering chocolate on page 24. Reserve 1 tablespoon of either the milk or dark chocolate for piping, then on the tines of a dipping or dinner fork, dip the hearts, one at a time, into either chocolate and allow any excess to drip back into the bowl. Carefully place the chocolate-coated hearts on clean parchment paper and decorate with crystallized roses or sprinkles. Spoon the reserved chocolate into the piping bag, snip the end into a fine point, and pipe decorative lines, swirls, or dots over the hearts. Leave in a cool place until set.

This is a basic ganache mixture with a few added extras. If you'd rather keep things classic and simple, leave out the spices and add a tablespoon or two of brandy, rum, or Marc de Champagne to the cream instead. Pictured left on page 18.

Aztec Truffles

Makes 25–30

¾ cup heavy cream plus
   1 tablespoon
2 tablespoons brown sugar
1 large cinnamon stick
½ vanilla pod, split
½ teaspoon red pepper
   flakes
2 strips orange peel
pinch of salt
12oz dark chocolate

To coat
3oz dark chocolate, grated

Store
The truffles will keep in an airtight box in the fridge for up to 1 week. Bring to room temperature to serve.

Place the cream in a small saucepan and add the brown sugar, cinnamon stick, vanilla pod, red pepper flakes, and strips of orange peel. Add the salt and heat gently until the cream is hot but not boiling. Remove from the heat and leave to infuse for at least 1 hour.

Finely chop 7 ounces of the chocolate and put into a bowl. Gently reheat the cream mixture until boiling and strain though a fine sieve onto the chocolate. Leave for 1 minute and then stir to combine into a smooth ganache. Leave to cool and then cover and chill until firm.

Using a teaspoon, scoop the ganache into cherry-sized balls and roll in your hands until smooth. Arrange on a parchment paper-covered tray and chill again for 15 minutes while you melt the remaining chocolate in a heatproof bowl over a pan of barely simmering water, making sure the bottom of the bowl doesn't touch the water. Stir until smooth and remove the bowl from the pan.

Put the grated chocolate on a large dinner plate or baking sheet. Spoon a teaspoon of the melted chocolate into the palm of one hand, drop a truffle into the chocolate and, using the other hand, roll it to coat all over. Drop the truffle into the grated chocolate and roll again to cover completely. Repeat with the remaining truffles and leave to set firm before serving.

These truffles are delicately scented with hints of bergamot and orange and hand-rolled in chocolate to coat. This can get messy so it might be an idea to enlist a pair of helping hands at this point in the proceedings. If you prefer, you can go down the neater, but less fun route, and simply dip the truffles into the chocolate using a dipping or dinner fork. Pictured right on page 19.

Earl Grey Tea Truffles

Makes 25–30

1 rounded tablespoon Earl Grey or jasmine tea leaves
1½ tablespoons superfine sugar
2 strips orange peel
7oz dark chocolate
a few drops bergamot oil (optional)
2 tablespoons heavy cream
small pinch of salt

To coat

5oz dark chocolate, chopped
2–3 tablespoons confectioner's sugar (or cocoa)

Store

The truffles will keep for up to 1 week in an airtight box in the fridge. Bring to room temperature to serve.

To make the ganache, measure ⅔ cup water into a small saucepan, add the tea leaves, sugar, and orange peel, and slowly bring to a boil to dissolve the sugar. Remove the pan from the heat and leave to cool for at least 1 hour to allow the tea to infuse the syrup.

Finely chop the chocolate and place in a bowl with the bergamot oil (if using). Add the cream and salt to the tea syrup and bring slowly back to a boil over medium heat. Simmer for 20 seconds and then strain into the chopped chocolate. Leave for 1 minute for the chocolate to melt in the residual heat of the syrup and then stir until smooth. Leave to cool, and then cover and chill until firm.

Using a teaspoon, scoop the ganache into cherry-sized balls and roll in your hands until smooth. Arrange on a parchment-covered tray and chill again for 15 minutes.

For the coating, melt the chocolate in a heatproof bowl over a pan of barely simmering water, making sure the bottom of the bowl doesn't touch the water. Stir until smooth and remove from the heat. Spread the confectioner's sugar (or cocoa) on a large dinner plate. Take 1 teaspoon of the melted chocolate and spoon it into the palm of one hand and roll one truffle in the chocolate to coat. Drop the truffle into the confectioner's sugar or cocoa and roll it around so that it is completely covered. Repeat with the remaining truffles, lightly shaking off the excess confectioner's sugar, and leave the truffles in a cool place to harden before serving.

Here's a fun way to serve truffles. I love the combination of peanut butter and raspberry puree; add chocolate to the mix and it's a winning formula. If you don't have lollipop sticks, these truffles can simply be sprinkled with raspberry dust or finely chopped peanut praline and served as they are. Pictured right on page 19.

Peanut and Raspberry Truffle Pops

Makes about 25

⅓ cup superfine sugar
plus 1 tablespoon
⅔ cup salted roasted
peanuts
5oz fresh raspberries
6oz dark chocolate,
chopped
3oz milk chocolate,
chopped
¾ cup heavy cream plus
1 tablespoon
1 teaspoon vanilla extract
or ½ teaspoon vanilla
bean paste
1 tablespoon unsweetened
peanut butter

To coat

7oz dark chocolate,
chopped

Equipment

lollipop sticks (optional)

Store

Truffle Pops will keep in an airtight box in the fridge for up to 1 week. Bring to room temperature to serve.

Tip the ⅓ cup superfine sugar into a small saucepan, add 2–3 teaspoons water, and set over low heat to dissolve the sugar without stirring. Bring the syrup to a boil and cook over medium heat until it turns into a honey-colored caramel. This will take no time at all due to the small quantity. Add the peanuts and stir to coat. Transfer the mixture to nonstick parchment paper and set aside to cool and harden.

Once the praline has completely cooled, finely chop either in a food processor or by hand using a kitchen knife.

Combine the raspberries and remaining 1 tablespoon superfine sugar in a small saucepan and cook over low-medium heat until the berries are very soft and juicy. Continue to cook gently for 10 minutes or so until the raspberry puree has reduced by half. Pass the puree through a fine mesh sieve, discarding the seeds. You should have roughly 2 tablespoons of thick, seedless raspberry puree.

Combine the dark and milk chocolate in a medium-sized bowl. Heat the heavy cream and vanilla extract or paste in a small pan until boiling and simmer gently for 30 seconds. Pour the hot cream over the chocolate, add the peanut butter and raspberry puree, and stir gently until combined and smooth. Leave to cool slightly, then add half of the peanut praline and stir gently to combine.

Leave the ganache to cool, cover and chill for at least 2 hours until firm, then using a teaspoon scoop the ganache into large cherry-sized balls and roll in your hands until smooth. If using lollipop sticks, push one into the middle of each truffle. Chill again for 30 minutes.

Meanwhile, put the dark chocolate into a heatproof bowl and melt over a pan of barely simmering water, making sure the bottom of the bowl doesn't touch the water. Stir until smooth. Remove from the heat and cool slightly. Dip one Truffle Pop at a time into the melted chocolate to coat, and allow the excess chocolate to drip back into the bowl. Press the top of the truffle into the remaining peanut praline and leave to set on parchment paper.

These are probably my favorite truffles—I love the contrast between the creamy, subtle caramel, rich (but not too rich) ganache, and the crisp dark-chocolate coating. When using cocoa for dusting, please make sure that it is one of superior quality. Pictured center on pages 18-19.

Sea-salted Caramel Truffles

Makes about 30–40

5oz milk chocolate, finely
  chopped
5oz dark chocolate, finely
  chopped
¼ cup superfine sugar
½ cup heavy cream
¼ cup brown sugar
1oz unsalted butter
1 teaspoon vanilla extract
  or ½ teaspoon vanilla
  bean paste
large pinch of sea salt flakes

To coat
7oz dark chocolate,
  chopped
1 cup cocoa

Equipment
7-inch square baking pan

Store
Store the truffles for up to
1 week in the fridge in an
airtight container between
layers of parchment paper.
Bring truffles to room
temperature to serve.

Line the baking pan with plastic wrap or nonstick parchment paper.

Combine the milk and dark chocolate in a medium-sized mixing bowl and set aside.

Place the superfine sugar in a small saucepan and add 2-3 teaspoons water. Set over low-medium heat to dissolve the sugar without stirring. Bring to a boil and continue to cook the syrup until it becomes an amber-colored caramel. This will take no time at all due to the small quantity. Remove the pan from the heat, add the heavy cream, brown sugar, butter, and vanilla extract or paste. Return to low heat to remelt the caramel if it hardened. Stir until smooth and bring to a boil. Pour the hot caramel cream into the chopped chocolate, add the salt, stir briefly, then leave to melt for 2-3 minutes. Beat the ganache until smooth and pour into the prepared pan and spread level with an offset spatula. Leave to cool, then cover and chill until firm for at least 3 hours.

To coat, melt the chocolate in a heatproof bowl placed over a pan of barely simmering water, making sure the bottom of the bowl doesn't touch the water. Stir until smooth, remove from the heat, and cool slightly. Spread the cocoa in a small roasting pan or on a large dinner plate.

Remove the ganache from the pan, peel off the plastic wrap or parchment and, using a hot kitchen knife, cut the ganache into bite-sized rectangular truffles. Drop two or three at a time into the melted chocolate and turn to cover on all sides. Using either a dipping or dinner fork, lift the truffles from the melted chocolate, tapping the fork on the side of the bowl to allow any excess to drip back into the bowl. Immediately drop the truffles into the cocoa, turn to coat on all sides, and leave to set for 4-5 minutes. Shake any excess cocoa off the truffles before serving.

These truffles have a few finishing stages—all of which I think are worth the effort; you can serve the unadorned truffles simply rolled in (good-quality) cocoa; you could stop after rolling them in the chopped pistachios; or you could go the whole hog, do as I do, and enrobe the nut-crusted truffles in white chocolate.

Look out for blanched pistachios in specialist grocery stores—their vibrant green color makes all the difference here. If you can't find them, simply blanch regular pistachios in boiling water for 30 seconds then drain them, and the skins should slip off between your fingers. Leave the nuts to dry thoroughly on paper towels before chopping.

Passion Fruit and Pistachio *Truffles*

Makes 25–30

4–6 passion fruits
8oz dark chocolate, chopped
⅓ cup heavy cream plus 2 tablespoons
1oz unsalted butter
1 tablespoon superfine sugar
½ teaspoon vanilla bean paste
pinch of salt
¾ cup blanched, unsalted pistachios
5oz good-quality white chocolate, chopped

Store
The truffles will keep in an airtight container in the fridge for up to 1 week.

Cut the passion fruits in half and scoop the flesh and juice into a sieve placed over a medium-sized heatproof bowl. Push the fruit through the sieve, extracting as much juice as possible, and discard the black seeds. You should have about 3 tablespoons of juice. Add the dark chocolate, cream, butter, sugar, vanilla, and salt, and set the bowl over a pan of barely simmering water. Do not allow the bottom of the bowl to touch the water. Melt the chocolate and butter into the cream, stirring from time to time until smooth. Remove from the heat and mix until silky smooth. Leave the ganache until cold, cover with plastic wrap, and chill for a couple or hours or until firm.

Meanwhile, finely chop the pistachios—I find this easiest in a mini-processor. Spread the nuts on a plate.

Using your hands, roll the chocolate truffle mixture into cherry-sized balls and then roll each truffle in the chopped pistachios so that they are coated in green nutty jackets. Chill the truffles for 15 minutes.

Melt the white chocolate in a heatproof bowl over a pan of barely simmering water, making sure the bottom of the bowl doesn't touch the water. Stir until smooth, remove from the heat, and cool slightly. Take a heaping teaspoon of melted white chocolate and pour it into the palm of your hand. Taking one truffle at a time, roll it into the melted chocolate to coat. Place the coated truffles on a clean sheet of nonstick parchment paper and leave in a cool place to allow the chocolate to set firm before serving.

To flavor these truffles I infuse the ganache with edible dried rose petals, often used in Middle-Eastern cuisine. They are available from ethnic grocers, good delis, or online. This ganache differs from most other recipes in that it is made with syrup rather than cream. This gives a smooth, clean taste that allows the delicate rose flavor to shine through without being overpowered.

Traditional rose creams, made with rose-flavored fondant and coated in dark chocolate, are slightly out of fashion these days, although they are still a particular favorite of mine and remind me of my grandmother and Great Auntie Biddy. This is my more modern take on the traditional rose cream and one that I'd like to think they would approve of.

Rose *Truffles*

Makes about 20

1 tablespoon dried rose
  petals
⅓ cup superfine sugar
12oz dark chocolate
  (64 percent cocoa solids),
  finely chopped
2–3 drops rose oil, organic
  and food safe (optional)
crystallized rose petals

Equipment
7-inch square baking pan
chocolate tempering
  thermometer
1-inch round cutter

Store
In a cool place for
1 week between sheets
of parchment paper in
an airtight box.

Start by making the rose-infused syrup. Place the rose petals in a small saucepan with the sugar and ½ cup water and heat gently to dissolve the sugar. Bring to a boil, simmer for 1 minute, and then pour the syrup and petals into a bowl and leave to cool. Cover and leave overnight so that the petals impart as much flavor into the syrup as possible.

Line the baking pan with plastic wrap or nonstick parchment paper. Place 7 ounces of the chocolate in a mixing bowl. Strain the syrup into a small saucepan (discarding the petals) and add the rose oil, if using. Gently heat the syrup until just boiling, then pour into the chocolate. Leave undisturbed for a couple of minutes, then stir until silky smooth. Pour the ganache into the prepared pan, spread level with an offset spatula, and leave until cold before covering and chilling until firm.

Temper the remaining chocolate according to the instructions below.

Turn the ganache out of the pan onto a board covered in parchment paper. Using the cutter, stamp out round truffles from the ganache block. Any scraps can be rolled into balls in your (clean) hands.

Taking one truffle at a time, place it on the tines of a dipping or dinner fork and submerge into the tempered chocolate. Lift the truffle from the chocolate, tap the tines of the fork on the side of the bowl, and allow the excess chocolate to drip back into the bowl. Carefully slide the truffle off the fork and onto a clean sheet of parchment. Top with a piece of crystallized rose and repeat with the remaining truffles. Leave the truffles to set firm before packaging.

Tempering chocolate
Put 3 ounces of the remaining chocolate in a heatproof bowl and place over a pan of barely simmering water, making sure the bottom of the bowl doesn't touch the water. Pop the tempering thermometer into the chocolate. Melt the chocolate, stirring until it is smooth and the chocolate reaches a temperature of 120°F. Remove the bowl from the pan, add the remaining chocolate, and stir to combine. Leave to cool to a temperature of 80°F, stirring frequently to speed up the cooling process. Return the bowl to the pan of hot water and reheat the chocolate to 88°F. Please note these temperatures are for dark chocolate only.

attempt to fly. Successful ... by the

5928 5927

RESERVED SEAT RESERVED SEAT

3/6/48 3/6/48

5927

5927

5927

Serve these rich, sophisticated bite-sized truffles after dinner with coffee. If you were feeling frugal—and clever—you could first make the Orangettes on page 96 and then use the leftover juice to make these truffles. If you want to take them to another level, and blood oranges happen to be in season, I urge you to use them—bitter caramel and blood-orange juice is a marriage made in heaven; add to that some good-quality chocolate and you've got yourself one really fancy truffle.

Bitter Orange Chocolate *Truffles*

Makes about 30

¼ cup superfine sugar
juice of 3 oranges (to yield
    ¾ cup)
9oz dark chocolate, finely
    chopped
⅓ cup heavy cream plus
    2 tablespoons
2 teaspoons brown sugar
pinch of salt
2 tablespoons finely
    chopped candied orange
    peel (preferably
    homemade Orangettes—
    see page 96)
cocoa powder for dusting

Equipment
7-inch square baking pan

Store
The truffles will keep for
up to 1 week between
layers of parchment paper
in an airtight container in
the fridge. Bring to room
temperature to serve.

Line the baking pan with nonstick parchment paper.

Tip the superfine sugar into a small saucepan and add 2–3 teaspoons water. Set the pan over low to medium heat to dissolve the sugar. Bring to a boil and cook steadily until the syrup turns into an amber-colored caramel, swirling the pan to ensure that the caramel cooks evenly. (This will not take long—a couple of minutes at best.) Remove the pan from the heat and add the orange juice, being careful because it will splatter and hiss as the juice hits the hot caramel. Return the pan to the heat and stir to remelt the caramel into the juice. Continue to cook over medium heat to reduce the mixture by half, until you have ½ cup syrup remaining. Remove from the heat.

Meanwhile, place the chocolate into a bowl. Heat the heavy cream and brown sugar in a small saucepan until just boiling and the sugar has melted. Pour this into the chocolate, add a small pinch of salt, and stir gently until the chocolate has melted into the cream. Add the warm caramel orange juice and stir gently to combine. Add the candied orange peel and stir gently. Pour the mixture into the prepared pan, spreading level with an offset spatula. Leave to cool and then cover and chill for at least 2 hours or until firm.

To serve, dust the top of the truffle mixture with a light coating of cocoa and cut into small squares using a warm kitchen knife. Dip the knife into hot water and dry on paper towels in between each slice to make slicing easier and neater. Remember that these truffles are rich and so should be served in elegant cubes rather than huge slabs.

This Chocolate Salami, also called *Salame al Cioccolato* or *Salame de Chocolate*, is traditionally either an Italian or Portuguese recipe, depending on where your allegiance lies. The fruit and nuts are interchangeable subject to your tastes and what treasures you have stashed in your pantry.

Chocolate Salami

Makes 2 salami and serves 20

⅓ cup golden raisins

½ cup dried figs, chopped into raisin-sized pieces

2 tablespoons dark rum or amaretto

1¼ cups mixed nuts (pistachios, blanched almonds, and hazelnuts)

7oz dark chocolate, chopped

3oz unsalted butter

⅓ cup superfine sugar

2 tablespoons brown sugar

1 large egg plus 1 large egg yolk

6oz plain cookies (such as amaretti or graham crackers)

2 tablespoons confectioner's sugar

Store

Chocolate Salami will keep for up to 1 week, well wrapped and in the fridge.

Preheat the oven to 350°F.

Put the golden raisins and figs in a medium bowl. Add 1 tablespoon of the rum or amaretto, mix well, and leave to soak while you prepare the remaining ingredients.

Put all of the nuts on a baking sheet and toast in the oven for about 4 minutes until lightly golden. Allow the nuts to cool slightly and then roughly chop.

Combine the chocolate and butter in a medium-sized heatproof bowl and melt over a pan of barely simmering water, taking care not to allow the bottom of the bowl to come into contact with the water. Stir until smooth. Meanwhile, in another bowl, whisk together the superfine sugar, brown sugar, whole egg, and egg yolk until smooth and thoroughly combined. Add to the chocolate and butter mixture and mix well. Stirring frequently, continue to cook over the pan of water until the sugar has dissolved, the mixture is silky smooth and hot to the touch, and the eggs are cooked—this will take about 4–5 minutes.

Meanwhile put the cookies in a freezer bag and crush using a rolling pin until the pieces are slightly larger than the golden raisins. Sprinkle with the remaining tablespoon of rum. Add the nuts and cookies to the dried fruit. Add to the chocolate mixture and stir with a rubber spatula to thoroughly combine. Leave at room temperature to cool and thicken slightly.

Take two large sheets of parchment paper and divide the mixture evenly between them, spreading it into a log. Roll the paper up and over the mixture, twisting the ends to seal and to pack the mixture into a tight sausage shape. Chill overnight.

Remove the salami from the fridge and unwrap from the paper. Spread the confectioner's sugar on a baking sheet and roll each salami in the sugar to coat completely. Using a sharp knife, cut the salami into slices to serve.

Soft, delicately flavored nougat, topped with creamy vanilla caramel and enrobed in chocolate, these are my much more sophisticated take on a popular candy bar and are the stuff of dreams. They do take a little time and effort, but are well worth it, both for the taste and the sheer wow factor. I would suggest making the nougat and caramel layers on one day and coating them in chocolate the next.

Be warned—these are rich!

Caramel Nougat Bars

Makes about 20

For the chocolate nougat
1 large egg white
1 teaspoon vanilla extract
1¼ cups superfine sugar
pinch of salt
1 tablespoon malted
   milk powder
4oz dark chocolate,
   chopped
¾ cup corn syrup

For the caramel
⅓ cup superfine sugar
⅓ cup brown sugar
2½ tablespoons corn syrup
2oz unsalted butter
⅓ cup heavy cream plus
   2 tablespoons
½ vanilla pod, split in half
a pinch of sea salt flakes

To coat
7oz dark chocolate,
   chopped
7oz milk chocolate,
   chopped
chocolate sprinkles or
   nonpareils, optional

Equipment
8 x 12-inch baking pan with
   a depth of 2 inches
sugar thermometer
disposable piping bag

Line the base and sides of the baking pan with nonstick parchment paper.

Place the egg white, vanilla extract, 1 tablespoon of the superfine sugar, and the salt in the bowl of a free-standing mixer fitted with a whisk attachment. Sift the malted milk powder into a small bowl. Melt the dark chocolate in a heatproof bowl over a pan of barely simmering water, making sure the bottom of the bowl doesn't touch the water. Stir until smooth and set aside.

Put the remaining superfine sugar and corn syrup into a medium-sized, heavy-bottomed saucepan and add ⅓ cup water. Warm over medium heat to dissolve the sugar, stirring from time to time. Pop the thermometer into the pan, bring to a boil, and continue to cook steadily over medium heat until the syrup reaches 257°F. Remove the pan from the heat and immediately start to whisk the egg-white mixture until stiff peaks form. With the mixer running on a slow–medium speed, pour the hot syrup into the egg white in a steady, continuous stream. The mixture will double or triple in volume at this point. Increase the speed to medium–high and continue to whisk for about 4 minutes, until the nougat has turned a pale creamy color and has cooled and thickened. Add the malted milk powder and the melted chocolate and whisk for another 10 seconds to combine. Using a rubber spatula and an offset spatula, work quickly to spoon the mixture into the prepared pan and spread level. Leave until cold.

For the caramel, combine both of the sugars, the corn syrup, butter, cream, vanilla pod, and sea salt flakes in a small, heavy-bottomed saucepan and set the pan over low–medium heat. Stir constantly to dissolve the sugars and melt the butter. Pop the sugar thermometer into the pan, bring the mixture to a steady boil, and continue to cook until the caramel reaches 244°F, then immediately remove the pan from the heat. Using tongs or a fork, remove the vanilla pod from the pan and pour the caramel over the nougat in an even layer. Leave to cool.

Once the caramel is completely cold, cover the pan in plastic wrap and set aside to set firm. Place in the fridge for 30 minutes while you prepare the chocolate coating. Draw an 8 x 12-inch rectangle on a sheet of nonstick parchment paper

Recipe continued overleaf

Store
These bars keep for
up to 1 week in an
airtight container in the
fridge—bring to room
temperature to serve.

and flip the paper over onto a baking sheet or board, so that you can see the lines you've drawn through the paper. Combine the dark and milk chocolate in a medium heatproof bowl and melt over a pan of barely simmering water, making sure the bottom of the pan doesn't touch the water. Stir until smooth and thoroughly combined and leave to cool to room temperature.

Remelt the chocolate until it becomes runny and glossy again. Using a spatula, spread 3 tablespoons of the melted chocolate over the parchment paper rectangle to cover it in an even layer. Turn the caramel nougat out of the pan onto a sheet of parchment paper, caramel side down, peel off the parchment paper, and quickly flip it back onto the chocolate rectangle, nougat side down. Pop the baking sheet into the fridge for 5 minutes to harden the chocolate. Take a long, sharp knife, heat the blade in a pitcher of hot water, dry the knife with paper towels, and trim the edges of the caramel nougat (these scraps are the cook's perks). Cut the square into 20 fingers or rectangles, heating the knife between slices.

Arrange the bars on a cooling rack set over a clean baking sheet. You will find it easier to coat the bars in chocolate in batches of 4 or 5 at a time, keeping the chocolate warm as you work. Using a teaspoon, carefully spoon the melted chocolate over each bar to coat the top and sides evenly. Using a spatula, carefully lift the bars off the cooling rack onto a clean sheet of parchment paper. Scoop about 2 tablespoons of the melted chocolate into a disposable piping bag, snip the end into a fine point, drizzle lines over each chocolate bar, and scatter with round chocolate sprinkles or chocolate nonpareils. Repeat with the remaining bars and chocolate, returning the chocolate that has drizzled onto the baking sheet to the bowl and remelting between batches if necessary. Leave to set completely before serving.

I was stopped in my tracks by a tray of these beauties in a chocolate shop in Copenhagen—I just had to try one to discover what was lurking beneath that crisp coating of dark chocolate. I have made them here somewhat smaller than is traditional—the Danish Flødeboller are a little on the large size, even for me. They are not the easiest morsel to devour elegantly—but elegance and a mountain of chocolate-coated meringue hardly go hand in hand anyway.

Flødeboller

Makes 20–24

confectioner's sugar,
  for dusting
10oz marzipan (see page
  48), or use store-bought
¼ cup finely chopped
  almonds or pistachios
¾ cup superfine sugar
3 large egg whites
pinch of salt
½ teaspoon vanilla bean
  paste
14oz dark chocolate,
  chopped
shredded coconut, chopped
  nuts, or freeze-dried
  raspberries (optional)

Equipment
2-inch plain cookie cutter
sugar thermometer
  (optional)
large piping bag fitted with
  a plain ½-inch nozzle

Store
These will keep for 3–4 days
in a cool place in an airtight
container.

Preheat the oven to 325°F and line a baking sheet with nonstick parchment paper.

Lightly dust the work surface with confectioner's sugar and roll the marzipan out ¼ inch thick. Sprinkle with the almonds or pistachios and give the marzipan a few more turns of the rolling pin—just enough to press the nuts into it. Using the cookie cutter, cut out as many rounds as you can from the marzipan and arrange them on the lined baking sheet. Gather the marzipan scraps together, re-roll, and cut out more rounds. Bake the marzipan bases on the middle shelf of the oven for about 5 minutes until golden. Remove from the oven and leave to cool.

Combine the superfine sugar, egg whites, and salt in a medium-sized, heatproof bowl. Add 2 tablespoons of water and set over a saucepan of simmering water. The bowl should fit snugly into the pan without touching the water (if it does, you run the risk of scrambling the egg whites). Whisking constantly, cook until the sugar has dissolved and the mixture has at least doubled in volume and is glossy, very white, and thick enough to hold a ribbon trail. This will take at least 4 minutes and the mixture should be hot to the touch or reach 140°F on a sugar thermometer. Add the vanilla and mix well. Scoop the meringue into the bowl of a free-standing mixer and whisk on medium–high speed for 3 minutes until very thick and cooled.

Spoon the meringue into the prepared piping bag and pipe generous mounds on top of each marzipan disk. Leave the meringues to dry for at least 1 hour.

Put two-thirds of the chocolate in a heatproof mixing bowl and melt over a pan of barely simmering water. Do not allow the bottom of the bowl to touch the water. Once the chocolate is smooth, remove from the heat, add the remaining chocolate, stir well, and leave to cool for about 15 minutes. Return the bowl to the pan for 10-15 seconds to warm through.

Taking one Flødebolle at a time, dip the underside of the marzipan base into the melted chocolate and then quickly and carefully dip the meringue top in so that it is completely coated on all sides. You may find it easier (and messier) to hold the Flødeboller over the bowl and spoon the chocolate over it. Allow any excess chocolate to drip back into the bowl and then return the chocolate-coated Flødeboller to the baking sheet to set for a minute. Sprinkle the top with coconut, chopped nuts, or freeze-dried raspberries if you like. Repeat with the remaining Flødeboller. Resist the temptation to eat one before the chocolate hardens!

It's hard to resist the combination of peanut butter and chocolate; it's one of those marriages made in foodie heaven. Here's my quick take on a much-loved classic. I've chosen not to temper the chocolate in this instance, but feel free to do so if you're after a more classy treat. But whichever way you make these, as always, use the best chocolate that you can lay your hands on.

Peanut Butter Cups

Makes 12–16 mini-muffin sized cups

2oz white chocolate, chopped
⅓ cup crunchy peanut butter
1 teaspoon vanilla extract
5oz milk chocolate, finely chopped
5oz dark chocolate, finely chopped
3 tablespoons finely chopped salted peanuts

Equipment
24-hole mini-muffin pan
pretty paper or foil mini-muffin cases

Store
Peanut Butter Cups will keep for 1 week in an airtight box in a cool place.

Line the mini-muffin pan with paper cases.

Start by preparing the peanut-butter filling. Put the white chocolate in a small heatproof bowl and melt either in 10-second blasts in the microwave on a low setting, or over a pan of barely simmering water, making sure the bottom of the bowl doesn't touch the water. Remove from the heat, stir until smooth, and add the peanut butter and vanilla extract. Mix to combine and set aside.

Place the milk and dark chocolate in a heatproof bowl and melt over a pan of barely simmering water, stirring frequently until silky smooth. Remove from the heat and cool slightly. Spoon 1 teaspoon of the melted chocolate into each paper case, then spoon roughly 1 level teaspoon of the peanut butter and white chocolate mixture into each cup, flattening the mixture slightly with the back of the spoon. Cover the peanut butter with another teaspoon of melted chocolate and tap the pan gently on the work surface, so that the chocolate covers the peanut butter in a smooth layer.

Sprinkle the peanuts over the top of each chocolate cup and leave in a cool spot until completely firm before serving.

This is my homage to the Australian Cherry Ripe chocolate bar. I spent a few happy weeks driving from Sydney to Cairns up the Australian east coast and a bag of mini Cherry Ripe bars was never far from my side. Sadly, Cherry Ripes are hard to come by elsewhere in the world so, when the need strikes, I make my own.

The chocolate cherry stalks for these truffles are optional but I think the extra effort is entirely worthwhile. The same goes for the sprinkling of freeze-dried cherry powder, available in specialist grocery stores or online.

Cherry Coconut Bombs

Makes about 25

1½ cups unsweetened dried coconut, plus a little extra
½ teaspoon coconut or vanilla extract
½ cup candied cherries
½ cup condensed milk
½ cup confectioner's sugar
9oz dark chocolate, finely chopped
freeze-dried cherry powder (optional)

Equipment
disposable piping bag

Store
Cherry Coconut Bombs will keep for 3–4 days in a cool place in an airtight box.

Put 1½ cups of the coconut in a mixing bowl and add 2 tablespoons of boiling water and the coconut (or vanilla) extract. Mix well until the coconut is softened (you may find it easiest to use your fingers for this), and set aside for 30 minutes.

If your candied cherries are very sticky and packed in a thick syrup, you'll need to give them a quick rinse in a sieve, then thoroughly pat dry on paper towels. Finely chop the cherries and add to the coconut along with the condensed milk and confectioner's sugar. Mix well with a wooden spoon until thoroughly combined.

Using your (clean) hands roll the coconut cherry mixture into about 25 even-sized balls and place on a parchment paper-covered baking sheet (this part can get sticky, so you'll find it easier if you rinse your hands after every 5 or 6 balls). Cover with plastic wrap and pop into the fridge to firm up for a good couple of hours.

Melt the chocolate in a heatproof bowl over a pan of barely simmering water, ensuring the bottom of the bowl does not come into contact with the water. Stir until the chocolate is smooth and remove from the heat. Scoop 2 tablespoons of the chocolate into a disposable piping bag and snip the end into a fine point. On a parchment paper-covered baking sheet, pipe the chocolate into stalk shapes, allowing one for each coconut bomb, plus a few extras in case of breakages. Chill in the fridge until firm.

Taking one coconut ball at a time, carefully drop it into the remaining melted chocolate and, using a fork, gently roll the ball around so that it is completely coated in chocolate. Lift out of the chocolate on the tines of the fork, tap the fork against the side of the bowl to allow any excess chocolate to drip back into the bowl, and gently place the bomb on a clean sheet of parchment paper. Repeat with the remaining bombs. Sprinkle the top of each bomb with dried coconut or freeze-dried cherry powder and carefully attach a chocolate stalk with a dot of melted chocolate. Leave until the chocolate is firm before serving.

In this recipe you will be making a small amount of nougat (small, but still loaded with almonds) and it is easiest to use a hand-held electric mixer rather than its larger freestanding cousin. It is even easier if you enlist another pair of hands to help with pouring the hot syrup and whisking the egg white, as these two things need to happen simultaneously. Pictured on page 43.

Chocolate Nougat Chunks

Makes enough for 8 greedy people

1¼ cups whole almonds (skin on)
1 medium egg white
pinch of cream of tartar
pinch of salt
¾ cup superfine sugar
1 tablespoon liquid glucose
⅓ cup honey
½ teaspoon vanilla bean paste or the seeds from ½ vanilla pod
10oz milk chocolate, chopped
4oz dark chocolate (64 percent cocoa solids), chopped

Equipment
sugar thermometer
8 x 12 inch baking sheet

Store
The nougat will keep for up to 4 days in an airtight box between layers of non-stick parchment paper.

Preheat the oven to 350°F.

Spread the almonds on a baking sheet and lightly toast in the oven for 3–4 minutes. Finely chop and leave to cool.

Place the egg white, cream of tartar, and salt in a medium-sized mixing bowl and place the bowl on a nonslip mat or damp towel.

Combine the superfine sugar, liquid glucose, and ¼ cup water in a small pan and stir gently over low heat to dissolve the sugar. Place the sugar thermometer in the pan and bring the syrup to a boil. Continue to cook until it reaches 320°F on the sugar thermometer. Meanwhile, heat the honey in a small saucepan or in a heatproof cup in the microwave until boiling. Slowly and carefully add the hot honey to the syrup, stirring well, and continue to cook until the syrup returns to 320°F. Remove the pan from the heat and, working quickly, whisk the egg white until stiff peaks form. Reduce the speed of the mixer to low and slowly pour about 1–2 tablespoons of the hot syrup into the egg white in a steady stream, whisking constantly. Add the remaining syrup in a slow, steady stream, whisking constantly. Add the vanilla, increase the speed to medium, and continue to whisk for another 2 minutes until the mixture is very thick and a pale buttermilk color. Add the chopped almonds right away and fold in using a rubber spatula.

Quickly scoop the mixture onto a large sheet of parchment paper and spread into an even layer using an offset spatula. Press another sheet of parchment paper on top of the nougat and use a rolling pin to flatten it to a thickness of a ¹⁄6th to ¹⁄8th of an inch. Leave for at least 4 hours until completely cold and firm.

Peel off the parchment paper and, using a kitchen knife, cut the nougat into small ¼-inch chunks. You will only need three-quarters of the nougat, so reserve the remainder and enjoy either as a cook's perk or stirred into vanilla ice cream.

Melt the milk and dark chocolate together in a heatproof bowl over a pan of barely simmering water, making sure the bottom of the bowl doesn't touch the water. Stir until smooth, remove from the heat and leave to cool slightly. Line the baking sheet with nonstick parchment paper.

Fold the chopped nougat into the melted chocolate and spoon onto the parchment paper. Spread level using an offset spatula and ensure that the nougat is evenly distributed. Leave until set firm before cutting into rough chunks to serve.

I like to give you options when I can, so in this recipe I'll leave it to you to decide whether you cover this salty caramel nutty confection in either milk or dark chocolate. Sometimes when I can't make up my mind which way to go in the chocolate department, I opt for a mixture of half milk and half dark. Children, however, may prefer the milk chocolate option. If you wanted to be really fancy, you could temper the chocolate for extra snap and shine, but sometimes it's nice to keep things simple.

Whichever route you go down, it'll be a hit. Pictured on page 42.

Almond Butterscotch Chocolate *Crunch*

Makes 30–40

1⅔ cups sliced almonds
1¼ cups superfine sugar
2oz unsalted butter
3 tablespoons heavy
    cream
½ teaspoon sea salt flakes
1 teaspoon vanilla extract
10oz dark (64 percent
    cocoa solids) or milk
    chocolate, finely chopped

Equipment
8 x 12 inch baking sheet

Store
These will keep in an airtight box between layers of parchment paper or wax paper for up to 1 week.

Preheat the oven to 350°F and line the baking sheet with nonstick parchment paper.

Spread the sliced almonds on a baking sheet and toast in the oven for about 5 minutes until lightly golden. Roughly chop the almonds and set aside.

Place the sugar in a medium-sized, heavy-bottomed saucepan and add 2 tablespoons of water. Place over low–medium heat to gently dissolve the sugar. If sugar crystals start to form on the sides of the pan, use a clean, wet pastry brush to dissolve them. Once the sugar has dissolved and the syrup is smooth, bring to a boil and continue to cook steadily, watching it like a hawk, until it turns into an amber-colored caramel. As always with boiling hot caramel you'll need to work quickly at this stage; remove the pan from the heat, add the butter and heavy cream, and stir until combined—the caramel will bubble furiously, so take care. Add the toasted almonds, salt flakes, and vanilla extract and return the pan to the heat for 30 seconds, stirring constantly until the caramel and nuts are combined. Scoop the mixture out of the pan into the prepared baking sheet, spread level with an offset spatula, and leave until completely cold and hardened.

Melt half the chocolate in a heatproof bowl set over a pan of barely simmering water, making sure the bottom of the bowl doesn't touch the water. Stir until smooth, then pour over the hardened almond brittle and spread evenly with an offset spatula. Tap the baking sheet gently on the work surface to level the chocolate and leave to cool until set and firm.

Melt the remaining chocolate, stir until smooth, and leave to cool slightly. Turn the cooled almond brittle out of the pan onto a clean sheet of parchment paper and peel off the lining paper. Spread the melted chocolate evenly over the brittle and leave until set before cutting into rough chunks to serve.

I adore these chocolate hearts, and what makes them even better in my book is that they are so easy to make, they barely require a recipe. You will, however, need to be snappy and catch the chocolate at the right moment: If you try to pipe it before it's firm enough, it will simply spread too much to hold a heart shape; and if it's too firm, it will be impossible to squeeze it out of the piping bag. This is the very reason that I suggest making small quantities at a time.

Valentine *Hearts*

Makes 6

¼–½ cup brightly colored cake decorating sprinkles
7oz dark chocolate, finely chopped

Equipment
disposable piping bag fitted with a small star shaped nozzle
6 colored ribbons

Store
The hearts will keep for up to 3 weeks in an airtight box in a cool place.

Scatter the sprinkles in an even layer on a parchment paper–covered baking sheet.

Put the chocolate in a heatproof bowl and place over a pan of barely simmering water, making sure the bottom of the bowl doesn't touch the water. Melt the chocolate, stirring until smooth, and then remove the bowl from the pan. Leave the chocolate to cool and thicken, stirring frequently, until it will just hold a ribbon trail, at which point you will need to move quickly.

Spoon the chocolate into the prepared piping bag and pipe heart shapes directly on top of the sprinkles. Leave until set firm, then thread each heart with colored ribbon.

You can reuse any leftover sprinkles either for cake decorating or to make more chocolate hearts.

As a child of the 1970s, I remember the days when fancy dark-chocolate mints were the height of sophistication. My mother almost always had a box lurking in a drawer to be served with coffee at dinner parties. However, that box would most likely be missing one or two chocolates—I could never resist a peppermint cream, not then and not now. I am also rather partial to violet and rose creams and often flavor homemade fondant with either violet or rose extract and top each chocolate with crystallized petals. They are deeply retro but I don't have a problem with that— they make me smile and I love them.

Peppermint Creams

Makes about 30

1¾ cups superfine sugar
1 tablespoon liquid glucose
a pinch of cream of tartar
½–1 teaspoon peppermint
    extract
confectioner's sugar, for
    dusting
7oz dark chocolate,
    chopped
crystallized mint leaves,
    to decorate

Equipment
sugar thermometer
1-inch square or round
    cookie cutter

Store
Peppermint Creams will
keep in a cool place for
1–2 weeks in an airtight
box between layers of
parchment paper.

Put the superfine sugar in a small saucepan and add the liquid glucose, cream of tartar, and ½ cup water. Slowly heat the mixture to dissolve the sugar, stirring from time to time. Pop the sugar thermometer into the pan, bring to a boil, and continue to cook steadily until the syrup reaches 238°F. Remove from the heat, pour into a medium-sized bowl, add the peppermint extract, and leave to cool at room temperature for 15–20 minutes, until the mixture has thickened with a skin covering the surface.

Using a hand-held electric mixer, beat the syrup until it thickens and becomes a smooth, thick, white paste. This will take about 3–5 minutes at slow-medium speed. You may need to turn the fondant out of the bowl once it starts to become very thick and doughlike and knead by hand until silky smooth and cold. Flatten the fondant into a disk, cover with plastic wrap, and chill for a few hours or overnight.

When ready to continue, lightly dust the work surface with confectioner's sugar and roll the fondant out to a thickness of a ¹/10th of an inch. Using the cookie cutter, cut out rounds or squares and place these on a parchment paper–lined baking sheet. Gather the trimmings together, knead until smooth, reroll, and cut out more shapes. Pop the sheet in the fridge to chill for 20 minutes while you melt the chocolate.

If you want your Peppermint Creams to have a more professional air about them, follow the instructions for tempering chocolate on page 24. Otherwise, simply melt the chocolate in a heatproof bowl over a pan of barely simmering water, making sure the bottom of the bowl doesn't touch the water. Stir until smooth, remove the bowl from the pan and cool slightly.

Using a dipping or dinner fork, submerge one fondant shape at a time into the melted chocolate, lift out, and tap the fork on the side of the bowl to allow the excess chocolate to drip back into the bowl. Carefully place a Peppermint Cream on a clean sheet of parchment paper, gently press the tines of the fork into the chocolate to make ridges on the surface, and scatter with crystallized mint leaves. Repeat with the remaining fondant shapes. Leave the Peppermint Creams to set firm before serving.

These elegant, grown-up delights are a chocolate-coated combination of homemade marzipan and candied orange peel. Although you could use store-bought marzipan and candied peel, it really will make a world of difference if you use homemade. For a twist, scatter the top of each chocolate with nibbed pistachios or a flicker of edible gold leaf. I like to use a small oval cutter to make these marzipans, but they would look equally beautiful as squares, rectangles or even hearts.

Marzipan and Orange Chocolates

Makes 20

confectioner's sugar, for
  rolling out
6oz marzipan (see below)
4 candied orange peels
  (see Orangettes, page 96)
7oz dark chocolate
chopped pistachios
  (optional)

Equipment
2-inch cookie cutter
disposable piping bag

Store
These chocolates will keep
for 1 week in an airtight
box, between layers of
parchment paper, in a cool
place.

Makes about 10oz
¾ cup superfine sugar
pinch of cream of tartar
⅓ cup blanched almonds
  or pistachios
1 cup ground almonds
1 large egg yolk
1 teaspoon finely grated
  lemon or orange zest
½ teaspoon almond extract
2 teaspoons brandy or
  Kirsch
1 teaspoon lemon juice
pinch of salt

Lightly dust the work surface with confectioner's sugar and roll out the marzipan to a thickness of a $1/10$th of an inch. Using the cookie cutter, cut out as many pieces as you can from the marzipan and arrange on a baking sheet lined with nonstick parchment paper. Gather the marzipan trimmings together, knead gently into a smooth ball, reroll, and then stamp out more shapes. You should have about 20 pieces in all. Pop the baking sheet in the fridge while you prepare the orange slivers and chocolate.

Finely slice the candied orange peels—you will need one strip for each piece of marzipan. Temper 5oz of the chocolate according to the instructions on page 24.

Using a fork, gently dip one piece of marzipan at a time into the melted chocolate and turn to coat. Lift the fork out of the chocolate, allowing any excess to drip back into the bowl, then slide the chocolate-coated marzipan back onto the parchment paper with the help of an offset spatula. Press a sliver of candied orange peel (and a piece pistachio, if using) on the top. Repeat with the remaining marzipan pieces and leave the chocolate to set completely.

Melt the remaining chocolate in a heatproof bowl over a pan of barely simmering water, ensuring that the bottom of the bowl doesn't touch the water. Stir until smooth and spoon into the disposable piping bag. Snip the tip of the bag into a fine point and drizzle the chocolate over the Marzipan and Orange Chocolates. Allow to set before packaging into bags or boxes.

To make your own marzipan
Put the sugar in a heavy-bottomed, small saucepan, and add the cream of tartar and ⅓ cup water. Stir gently to dissolve the sugar, pop a sugar thermometer into the pan, and bring the syrup to a boil. Continue to cook steadily until it reaches 245°F. Remove from the heat and leave to cool for 3–4 minutes.

Meanwhile process the almonds (or pistachios) in the food processor until finely ground and mix with the almond flour. Tip the nuts and the remaining ingredients into the pan and beat until smooth. Return to a low heat and cook for 2–3 minutes, stirring constantly to cook the egg and to thicken the almond paste. Scoop the marzipan into a bowl, cover with plastic wrap, and leave until cold.

Flatten the cooled marzipan into a disk, wrap in plastic wrap, and refrigerate until ready to use. It will last, well wrapped and in the fridge, for up to 3 weeks.

For this recipe you will need a small amount of ganache to fill the eggs. If you were planning to make any of the chocolate truffles in this chapter to give as Easter gifts alongside these eggs, just hold back 3 tablespoons of the ganache and use it as a filling. Failing that, you could fill the eggs with Nutella, dulce de leche, Peanut Butter Cup filling (see page 36), or simply extra melted white or milk chocolate. I use a mold that has holes each measuring 1⅓ inches from top to bottom.

Speckled Mini *Easter Eggs*

Makes 12

1oz white chocolate, chopped

7oz dark chocolate, chopped

3 tablespoons chocolate ganache (reserved from making chocolate truffles)

ment

e Easter egg mold

ish

tempering

eter

2 c   e piping bags

Store

Chocola   ill keep for up to 2 w   n an airtight box in a cool place.

Wash the egg mold in hot, soapy water and dry thoroughly using a lint-free cloth. Glass-cleaning cloths are ideal for this purpose.

Melt the white chocolate in a small heatproof bowl either in the microwave in short bursts on a low setting, or over a pan of barely simmering water, making sure the bottom of the bowl doesn't touch the water. Stir until smooth and using a clean, dry and preferably new craft brush, dapple the inside of each egg mold with the melted white chocolate. Leave to dry.

Temper the dark chocolate according to the instructions on page 24.

Lay the mold on a large sheet of parchment paper and spoon two-thirds of the melted dark chocolate into the mold, filling all of the egg shapes. Tilt the mold from side to side so that the inside of each egg is evenly coated. Hold the mold over the bowl of melted chocolate and use an offset spatula or dough scraper to scrape the excess chocolate cleanly away and back into the bowl, then turn the mold upside down and leave to drain over the parchment paper, elevating slightly by resting the ends on wooden spoons. Allow the chocolate shells to set until completely solid.

Melt the ganache in a heatproof bowl over a pan of barely simmering water. Stir until just smooth and pourable, but not hot. Spoon into one of the piping bags, snip the end into a point, and pipe the ganache neatly into each chocolate egg. Fill each half no more than two-thirds full and leave a gap of at least ¹⁄₁₆th of an inch from the top of the ganache to the top of eggshell. Tap the molds to level the surface of the ganache and pop in the fridge for 5 minutes until firm.

Remelt the reserved dark chocolate, stir until smooth, remove from the heat, and cool slightly. Spoon into the second piping bag, snip the end into a fine point, and pipe melted chocolate over the top of the ganache, filling the eggs neatly and resulting in a flat, smooth surface. Leave the eggs to set solid.

Once the eggs are solid, turn the mold over, holding it above a clean sheet of parchment paper. Gently press or tap the mold so that the eggs gently pop out. Neatly pipe a dot of melted chocolate onto the flat side of half of the eggs, then top each one with another half. Leave to set firm.

Chocolate *Bark*

Makes 1 large sheet

5oz dark chocolate
3oz milk chocolate
5oz white chocolate
1 cup chopped toasted nuts
(pecans, almonds and
hazelnuts)

Store
This will keep for 2 weeks in
an airtight box in the fridge.

Chop all the chocolate and melt the three kinds separately in heatproof bowls set over pans of barely simmering water, making sure the bottoms of the bowls don't touch the water. Stir until smooth, remove from the heat, and cool for 1 minute.

Line a large baking sheet with nonstick parchment paper, allowing the paper to come up the sides of the baking sheet.

Spoon the chocolate onto the parchment, alternating dark, milk, and white chocolate. Tap the baking sheet on the work surface so that the chocolate forms an even layer and, using the end of a blunt knife, swirl the chocolates together to create a marbled pattern. Tap the baking sheet again to level.

Sprinkle the nuts all over the chocolate and leave in a cool place or the fridge until set firm. Break the bark into pieces to serve.

Dazzle Drops

Makes about 40

5oz dark chocolate,
chopped
1 tablespoon candied
ginger, finely chopped
2 tablespoons dried mango
slices, cut into slivers
2-3 teaspoons edible gold
sugar balls
pinch of red pepper flakes
(optional)

Store
Dazzle Drops will keep for
2 weeks in an airtight box in
the fridge between sheets of
nonstick parchment paper.

Melt the chocolate in a heatproof bowl over a pan of barely simmering water, making sure the bottom of the bowl doesn't touch the water. Stir until smooth, remove from the pan and leave to cool for a minute or two.

Line a large baking sheet with nonstick parchment paper. If you want your Dazzle Drops to be neat and more uniform, then spoon the melted chocolate into a disposable piping bag, snip the end into a point and pipe chocolate buttons in neat rows on the parchment paper. For a more organic look, simply spoon the chocolate onto the paper using a teaspoon. Arrange the ginger and mango on top of each chocolate drop and scatter the edible gold balls and a flake or two of red pepper flakes, if using.

Leave until set firm before removing from the paper.

Homemade chocolate bars are fun to make, look divine, and taste delicious. What more could you want from an hour or so in the kitchen?

Silicone chocolate bar molds are readily available in a huge variety of shapes and sizes in good cookware stores or online. However, if you don't want or need any more equipment cluttering up your kitchen cupboards (I feel your pain), then simply use what you have on hand—mini or individual tart and cake pans lined with nonstick parchment paper serve the purpose just as well.

I love freeze-dried berries (if you hadn't already noticed)—they come in umpteen flavors, most of which, as luck would have it, pair beautifully with chocolate. You could also use nuts and dried fruit. Banana chips and shredded coconut, candied violet and rose petals, cake-decorating sprinkles, crystallized ginger, mini marshmallows, popcorn, dried red pepper flakes, spices... the list goes on. You can also try adding a drop of violet, rose, orange, lemon, or peppermint extract to the melted chocolate for an extra little flavor boost to your bars.

Chocolate *Bars*

Makes 3–4, depending on the size of your molds

7oz white, milk or dark chocolate

A mixture of
a small handful each of freeze-dried strawberry slices, freeze-dried raspberries and freeze-dried sliced cherries
1 tablespoon crystallized rose and violet chips

or
dried banana chips
toasted shredded coconut
chopped and toasted macadamias, almonds, or hazelnuts
raisins

Equipment
chocolate molds

Wash your molds in hot soapy water and dry thoroughly using a lint-free cloth. Glass-polishing cloths are ideal for this purpose.

Melt the chocolate in a heatproof bowl over a pan of barely simmering water, making sure the bottom of the bowl doesn't touch the water. Add a drop of extract, if using, and stir until smooth.

Pour or spoon the melted chocolate into the prepared molds, filling them neatly but leaving a narrow border at the top. Sprinkle with your choice of toppings, pressing any larger pieces into the chocolate so that they will stick.

Leave the chocolate bars to cool and harden completely before removing from the molds.

Note
For a professional finish to your bars, temper the chocolate following the instructions on page 24. However, if you are using flexible silicone molds, you will find that they give a shiny finish to the chocolate bars and so tempering is not always necessary.

Store
Chocolate bars will keep for 1–2 weeks in an airtight box in a cool place.

Hot chocolate on a spoon! You can make these as sophisticated or child-friendly as you see fit: Add a splash of brandy, dark rum, Cointreau, or Baileys to the melted chocolate and you've got (adult) hot chocolate with a hit; add marshmallows and chocolate sprinkles and you're checking boxes as far as the kids are concerned.

Hot Chocolate *Dunkers*

Makes about 12

7oz dark, milk or white
  chocolate
splash of chosen alcohol
  (optional)
finely chopped toasted
  almonds or hazelnuts
mini marshmallows
chocolate sprinkles

Equipment
12 paper mini muffin cases
12 wooden teaspoons or
  coffee stirrers

Store
These will keep for up
to 2 weeks in an airtight box
in a cool place.

Chop the chocolate and melt in a heatproof bowl set over a pan of barely simmering water, making sure the bottom of the bowl doesn't touch the water. Stir until smooth and remove from the heat. If you are making these for adults, now would be the time to add the alcohol.

Divide the melted chocolate among the paper cases. Push a spoon or stirrer into the middle of each dunker so that it stands upright, then scatter the chocolate with your choice of toppings.

Leave the dunkers to set solid before either wrapping in clear plastic as gifts or serving.

To serve, heat one mug of milk per dunker in a saucepan and whisk furiously until frothy. Pour into mugs, peel the paper off the dunkers, and drop the dunkers into the mugs of milk. Stir slowly until the chocolate melts, and drink immediately.

Marshmallows

Rosewater and Pistachio Marshmallows

Summer Berry Marshmallows

Blueberry Lemonade Marshmallows

Marshmallow Lollipops

Toasted Coconut Marshmallows

Gingerbread Marshmallows

Marbled Mocha Marshmallows

Double Dipped Marshmallows

*I*f you have never tried homemade marshmallows, then you are in for a treat. Little clouds of scented sugary air that melt in the mouth, not only are these marshmallows quick and fun to make, they are a million times better than any store-bought alternative. It's almost impossible to think of marshmallows without conjuring up thoughts of steaming mugs of hot chocolate, s'mores, or campfires, but they are so much more than that—marshmallows are my idea of sweet heaven.

Marshmallows are the fun and frivolous sweet cousins to more sophisticated chocolate truffles and sticky caramels; they can be made in a dazzling range of flavors, shapes, and colors. Vanilla-flecked, spiced, or flavored with fresh fruit puree, there is a marshmallow for everyone. In my experience, children love to help make them—however, a little adult supervision will be needed with boiling and pouring hot syrup.

I use sheet rather than powdered gelatin to make marshmallows, as it gives a cleaner, purer tasting result. It is now easily available in good supermarkets. All of the marshmallow recipes in this book have been tested using platinum-grade sheet gelatin (look for the Dr. Oetker brand).

Preparation is key when making marshmallows—I really do urge you to have all the different components ready to go before you commence with the notion of boiling sugar syrup and whisking eggs. These little babies wait for no man and when I say, "On your marks, get set, GO," I mean it!

Marshmallows can be simply cut into squares, stamped into shapes using greased cookie cutters, or piped into ropes and cut into lengths and twists. Any marshmallow scraps are delicious folded into melted chocolate with a good handful of chopped nuts to make rocky road or dropped into mugs of steaming hot chocolate. And here we are back at hot chocolate!

The beauty of these delicately fragranced marshmallows lies in their contrasting pink and vibrant green colors. It's worth seeking out blanched pistachios, which are available from Middle-Eastern supermarkets (while you are there, pick up a bottle of good quality rosewater) or online. If you can't find them, it is easy enough to skin pistachios yourself, and for this recipe I would seriously recommend that you do so; soak shelled, unsalted pistachios in boiling water for 1–2 minutes, then rub the skins off between your fingers. Leave the pistachios to dry on paper towels for at least 1 hour before using.

Rosewater and Pistachio Marshmallows

Makes about 30

½ cup blanched pistachios
2 tablespoons
   confectioner's sugar
2 tablespoons cornstarch
sunflower oil, for greasing
6 sheets platinum-grade
   gelatin
2 large egg whites
pinch of salt
1¾ cups superfine sugar
1 tablespoon liquid glucose
   (or corn syrup)
1–2 teaspoons rosewater
red or pink food
   coloring paste

Equipment
8 x 12 inch baking sheet
sugar thermometer

Store
The marshmallows will keep for up to 1 week in an airtight box.

Finely chop the pistachios in a food processor and set aside. Mix the confectioner's sugar and cornstarch together in a small bowl. Lightly grease the baking sheet with sunflower oil, then line with lightly greased nonstick parchment paper. Dust the confectioner's sugar mix over the parchment paper in an even layer and tip the excess back into the bowl.

Soak the gelatin sheets in a bowl of cold water for 10 minutes until soft and, meanwhile, prepare the remaining ingredients. Place the egg whites in the bowl of a free-standing mixer fitted with a whisk attachment, and add the salt and 1 tablespoon of the superfine sugar.

Tip the remaining superfine sugar and glucose into a medium-sized saucepan and add ⅔ cup water. Place over medium heat and stir gently to dissolve the sugar. Increase the heat and bring the mixture to a boil. Continue to cook at a steady boil until the syrup reaches a temperature of 248°F on a sugar thermometer. Remove the pan from the heat.

Drain the gelatin from the water and blot dry on a clean towel. Quickly whisk the egg whites until stiff peaks form. Still working quickly, add the gelatin to the hot syrup and stir until completely combined. With the mixer on medium speed, add the hot syrup to the whisked egg whites in a slow and steady stream. Avoid pouring the syrup directly on to the whisk as this will cause it to splatter onto the sides of the bowl instead of into the mixture. Continue to whisk for 3–4 minutes more, until the marshmallow is cool, very glossy white, and stiff enough to hold a firm ribbon trail when the whisk is lifted from the bowl. Add the rosewater and mix to combine. Add a tiny amount of food coloring and whisk until the marshmallow is evenly colored. Add more food coloring in small increments to reach your desired shade of pink—a little goes a long way. Scoop the marshmallow into the prepared pan and spread level with an offset spatula. Scatter with the pistachios and leave in a cool place for at least 2 hours until set. Cover with plastic wrap and leave for another 4 hours or overnight.

To serve, sift the reserved confectioner's sugar mix onto a large parchment-covered baking sheet. Carefully turn out the marshmallow onto it and peel off the lining paper. Using a greased kitchen knife, cut the marshmallow into delicate fingers, then roll the sides and bottom of each piece in the confectioner's sugar mix.

Cut into heart shapes, as pictured on page 62, using a lightly greased cookie cutter and packed into pretty boxes, these make wonderful wedding favors or Valentine's Day gifts. They will not keep as long as other flavors due to the fresh berry puree. However, I don't imagine that this will be too much of a problem, as they never seem to hang around for long in my experience.

Summer Berry Marshmallows

Makes about 40

2 tablespoons confectioner's sugar
2 tablespoons cornstarch
sunflower oil, for greasing
3 cups mixed strawberries and raspberries, trimmed
1¾ cups superfine sugar plus 2 tablespoons
½ teaspoon vanilla bean paste
2 teaspoons lemon juice
2 large egg whites
pinch of salt
6 sheets platinum-grade gelatin

Equipment
9-inch square baking pan
sugar thermometer
heart-shaped cutter (optional)

Store
Summer Berry Marshmallows will keep for 3–4 days in an airtight box.

Sift the confectioner's sugar and cornstarch together in a small bowl. Lightly grease the baking pan with sunflower oil and line with lightly greased nonstick parchment paper. Lightly dust the confectioner's sugar mix over the parchment in an even layer and tip the excess back into the bowl and set aside.

Cook the berries gently in a small saucepan with 1 tablespoon of the superfine sugar, the vanilla paste, and lemon juice over low to medium heat until they become really soft and juicy. Pour into a sieve and, using a wooden spoon, push the mixture through into a bowl. Discard the seeds and return the berry puree to the cleaned pan. Place over low heat and continue to cook, stirring frequently, until it reduces to a jammy consistency. Remove from the heat.

Place the egg whites in the bowl of a free-standing mixer fitted with a whisk attachment. Add the salt and 1 tablespoon of superfine sugar, but do not start to whisk yet. Soak the gelatin sheets in a bowl of cold water for 10 minutes.

Tip the 1¾ cups superfine sugar into a medium-sized saucepan and add ⅔ cup water. Set over low to medium heat to dissolve the sugar, stirring frequently. Bring to a boil and continue to cook steadily until it reaches 257°F on a sugar thermometer. Remove the pan from the heat. Now you have to do three things at once: Start whisking the egg whites on medium speed until they will just hold a stiff peak; warm the puree over low to medium heat; and drain the gelatin leaves and blot dry on a clean towel.

Add the gelatin to the hot syrup and whisk to combine. With the mixer on medium speed, add to the egg whites in a slow and steady stream. As the egg whites are cooked by the hot syrup they will rise up rather dramatically and double in volume. Add the berry puree and continue to whisk for another 3 minutes or so, until the mixture has cooled slightly, is very thick and glossy, and will hold a firm ribbon trail.

Scoop the mixture into the prepared pan and gently spread level with an offset spatula. Set aside until completely cold before covering with plastic wrap and leaving for at least 4 hours or overnight until set firm.

Scatter the reserved confectioner's sugar mixture onto a parchment-covered baking sheet. Carefully turn out the marshmallow onto it and peel off the lining paper. Using a greased kitchen knife, heart-shaped cutter, or pizza wheel, cut the marshmallow into bite-sized pieces and coat in the confectioner's sugar mixture.

I like to think of these pillowy, double layered delights as the marshmallow equivalent of a blueberry cream soda. Fresh blueberry marshmallow sits atop a layer of tangy, lemony lightness, or is it the other way around?

I apologize for the excessive use of bowls needed here—the results will be worth it, and I find that helpers are never in short supply when marshmallow making is on the agenda.

If you prefer not to make double-layer marshmallows, then simply mix the blueberry puree, lemon zest, and citric acid into the basic marshmallow mixture. The result will perhaps not be as pretty, but will certainly be no less delicious.

Blueberry Lemonade Marshmallows

Makes 20–30

2 tablespoons cornstarch
2 tablespoons confectioner's sugar
sunflower oil, for greasing
1 unwaxed lemon
1½ cups fresh blueberries
1¾ cups superfine sugar
½ teaspoon vanilla bean paste
6 sheets platinum grade sheet gelatin
2 large egg whites
pinch of salt
¼ teaspoon citric acid

Equipment
8-inch square baking pan
sugar thermometer
1-inch round cookie cutter (optional)

Store
The marshmallows will keep in an airtight box between layers of nonstick parchment paper for 3–4 days.

Mix the cornstarch and confectioner's sugar together in a small bowl. Lightly grease the baking pan with sunflower oil, line with nonstick parchment paper, then lightly grease this also and dust with the cornstarch and confectioner's sugar mixture. Tip the excess back into the bowl and set aside.

Finely grate the zest from the lemon and set aside. Squeeze the juice from one lemon half and place in a small saucepan with the blueberries and 1 tablespoon of the superfine sugar. Set over low heat and cook the blueberries until they burst and become very soft. Using an immersion blender, puree until smooth. Continue to cook, stirring frequently, until the puree has reduced to 3–4 tablespoons and is of a jammy consistency. Add the vanilla bean paste, remove from the heat and set aside.

Place the gelatin sheets in a medium-sized bowl, cover with cold water, and leave for 10 minutes. Tip the egg whites into the bowl of a mixer fitted with a whisk attachment, and add a pinch of salt and 1 tablespoon of superfine sugar.

Tip the remaining sugar into a medium saucepan, add ⅔ cup water and heat gently to dissolve the sugar. Bring the syrup to a boil, and continue to cook until it reaches 248°F on the sugar thermometer. Now you need to work quickly. Remove the syrup from the heat and start whisking the egg whites on a high speed until they hold a stiff peak. Drain the gelatin from the water and blot dry on a clean towel. Quickly add the softened gelatin leaves to the hot syrup and mix to combine using a rubber spatula. With the mixer running on low to medium speed, add the syrup to the egg whites in a slow, steady stream, being careful not to pour the syrup directly onto the whisk or it will splatter all over the sides of the bowl and not mix into the egg whites. Continue to whisk on medium to high speed for another 3 minutes until the mixture has cooled, doubled or tripled in volume, is very thick and glossy white, and will hold a ribbon trail when the whisk is lifted from the bowl.

Recipe continued overleaf

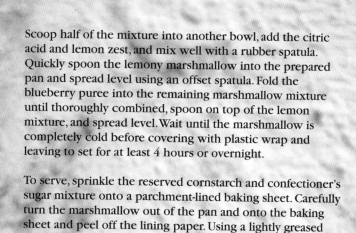

Scoop half of the mixture into another bowl, add the citric acid and lemon zest, and mix well with a rubber spatula. Quickly spoon the lemony marshmallow into the prepared pan and spread level using an offset spatula. Fold the blueberry puree into the remaining marshmallow mixture until thoroughly combined, spoon on top of the lemon mixture, and spread level. Wait until the marshmallow is completely cold before covering with plastic wrap and leaving to set for at least 4 hours or overnight.

To serve, sprinkle the reserved cornstarch and confectioner's sugar mixture onto a parchment-lined baking sheet. Carefully turn the marshmallow out of the pan and onto the baking sheet and peel off the lining paper. Using a lightly greased cutter or kitchen knife, cut the marshmallow into pieces and roll in the confectioner's sugar mix to coat.

These lollipops just make me smile. They are slightly crazy, really rather pretty, and the world is your marshmallow oyster when it comes to embellishments: You can leave them as a pure and white swirl, which I do like; you can drizzle them with melted white or dark chocolate; or you can go the whole hog and get out the sprinkles. Smiles all around.

Marshmallow *Lollipops*

Makes about 12

2 tablespoons
    confectioner's sugar
2 tablespoons cornstarch
6 sheets platinum-grade
    sheet gelatin
2 large egg whites
pinch of salt
1¾ cups superfine sugar
1 tablespoon liquid glucose
    (or corn syrup)
1 teaspoon vanilla bean
    paste or the seeds from
    ½ vanilla pod
1½oz dark chocolate,
    chopped
1½oz white chocolate,
    chopped
1 tablespoon sugar
    sprinkles

Equipment
12 lollipop sticks
sugar thermometer
2 large piping bags
½-inch plain nozzle
1 open star nozzle
2 disposable piping bags

Store
The marshmallow pops
will keep in an airtight box
for up to 1 week.

Line two large baking sheets with nonstick parchment paper. Mix the confectioner's sugar and cornstarch together in a small bowl and liberally dust the baking sheets with a thick, even layer. Arrange the lollipop sticks on the confectioner's sugar mixture (six per sheet), spacing them well apart.

Soak the gelatin sheets in a bowl of cold water for 10 minutes.

Place the egg whites in the bowl of a mixer fitted with a whisk attachment. Add the salt and 1 tablespoon of the superfine sugar, but don't whisk yet.

Tip the remaining superfine sugar and the glucose into a medium-sized saucepan and add ⅔ cup water. Place over medium heat and stir gently to dissolve the sugar. Raise the heat, and bring the mixture to a boil. Continue to cook at a steady boil until the syrup reaches a temperature of 248°F on a sugar thermometer. Remove the pan from the heat.

Drain the gelatin from the water and blot dry on a clean towel. Whisk the egg whites until stiff peaks form. Working quickly, add the gelatin to the hot syrup and stir until completely combined. With the mixer running on medium speed, add the hot syrup to the whisked egg whites in a steady stream. Add the vanilla and continue to whisk for 3–4 minutes until the mixture is cool, very glossy white, and stiff enough to hold a firm ribbon trail when the whisk is lifted from the bowl.

Fit one of the large piping bags with the plain nozzle and the other with the open star nozzle. Quickly divide the mixture between the two bags. Pipe tight spirals over one end of each of the lollipop sticks. Leave to set for 10 minutes, then lightly dust with a little of the confectioner's sugar and cornstarch mixture. Leave in a cool place for at least 4 hours until firm and set.

Melt the dark and white chocolate separately in bowls set over pans of barely simmering water, making sure the bottom of the bowl doesn't touch the water. Stir until smooth and spoon into disposable piping bags. Snip the tip of each bag into a fine point and drizzle the chocolate over the lollies with wild abandon. Scatter with sprinkles and leave to set before serving.

Toasted Coconut *Marshmallows*

Makes 30–40

¾ cup sweetened shredded
  coconut
sunflower oil, for greasing
1 tablespoon cornstarch
1 tablespoon confectioner's
  sugar
6 sheets platinum-grade
  sheet gelatin
2 large egg whites
1½ cups superfine sugar
½ teaspoon vanilla bean
  paste
pinch of salt
⅓ cup palm sugar or
  brown sugar
1 teaspoon natural coconut
  extract

Equipment

9-inch square baking pan
  with a depth of 1½ inches
sugar thermometer

Store

The marshmallows will keep
in an airtight container for
up to 1 week.

Tip the coconut into a dry frying pan, place over low heat, and toast until lightly golden, stirring frequently to prevent the coconut from scorching. Remove from the heat and set aside.

Lightly grease the pan with sunflower oil, line the base and sides with nonstick parchment paper, then lightly grease this also. In a small bowl mix together the cornstarch and confectioner's sugar. Transfer to a sieve and lightly dust the greased paper, tipping any excess out of the pan and back into the bowl. Sprinkle half of the toasted coconut over the base of the pan in an even layer.

Soak the gelatin leaves in a bowl of cold water for 10 minutes. Meanwhile, tip the egg whites into the bowl of a free-standing mixer fitted with a whisk attachment. Add 1 tablespoon of the superfine sugar, the vanilla bean paste, and salt, but do not start mixing yet.

Combine the palm sugar (or brown sugar) and the remaining superfine sugar in a saucepan, add ⅔ cup water, and warm over medium heat. Once the sugar has completely dissolved, bring the syrup to a boil and continue to cook steadily until the syrup reaches a temperature of 248°F on the sugar thermometer.

Now you need to work quickly. Remove the pan from the heat. Whisk the egg whites until stiff peaks form. Drain the softened gelatin from the water and quickly blot on a clean towel, then add, along with the coconut extract, to the hot syrup and stir quickly to incorporate. With the mixer running on slow to medium speed, add the hot syrup-gelatin mixture to the egg whites in a steady stream, being careful not to pour the syrup directly onto the whisk as it will splash up the sides of the bowl rather than mix into the egg whites. Once all of the syrup has been added, increase the speed to medium and continue to whisk for 3–4 minutes until the mixture is stiff, white and glossy, and easily holds a ribbon trail when the whisk is lifted from the bowl.

Using a rubber spatula and offset spatula, spoon the marshmallow into the prepared pan and spread in an even layer. Sprinkle with the remaining toasted coconut and leave to cool to room temperature. Cover with plastic wrap and leave for a good couple or hours or overnight until set completely.

Once set, carefully turn the marshmallow out of the pan onto a board and peel off the parchment paper. Using a greased kitchen knife, cut into evenly sized squares and toss in any loose coconut to prevent it from sticking together.

When it comes to the coconut coating for these marshmallows, you can go one of two ways. You can keep it easy and use dried coconut, which is readily available, or you can use sweetened, shredded coconut, which, as the name implies, is sweeter and has longer coconut pieces. Whenever I see the latter in specialty stores or online, I stock up on it, since it makes for a more dramatic coconut finish on candies and cakes. I've also used natural coconut extract in this recipe, which should not be confused with coconut flavoring—this is a different beast altogether, never having been anywhere near a real coconut.

Although these spiced marshmallows are quite scrumptious just as they are, sometimes you need to push the boat out—and when I say push the boat out, I mean right out. So get yourself a pack of fine cookies, a jar of dulce de leche (or any good toffee sauce), a bonfire, and perhaps a guitar for musical accompaniment. Spread a generous spoonful of toffee sauce over a cookie, toast the marshmallows over the fire, arrange the warm, melting marshmallows over the toffee sauce and sandwich with another cookie. Campfire cooking just got a whole lot more exciting.

Gingerbread Marshmallows

Makes about 30

sunflower oil, for greasing
2 tablespoons
   confectioner's sugar
2 tablespoons cornstarch
6 sheets platinum-grade
   gelatin
2 large egg whites
1 cup superfine sugar
pinch of salt
2 teaspoons ground ginger
½ teaspoon ground
   cinnamon
generous pinch of ground
   allspice
generous pinch of ground
   cloves
generous grating of
   nutmeg
½ cup brown sugar
2 tablespoons molasses
2 tablespoons corn syrup

Equipment
8-inch square baking pan
sugar thermometer

Store
The marshmallows will
keep for up to 1 week in an
airtight container.

Lightly grease the baking pan with sunflower oil, line with nonstick parchment paper, and lightly grease the parchment. In a small bowl combine the confectioner's sugar and cornstarch. Dust the inside of the lined pan with a tablespoon or so of the confectioner's sugar mix, tip the excess back into the bowl, and set aside.

Place the gelatin sheets in a bowl, cover with cold water, and leave to soak and soften while you prepare the rest of the ingredients.

Place the egg whites in the bowl of a free-standing mixer fitted with a whisk attachment. Add 1 tablespoon of the superfine sugar and the salt, but do not start whisking yet. Mix all of the spices together in a small bowl.

Combine the remaining superfine sugar, the brown sugar, molasses, and corn syrup in a medium-sized saucepan. Add ⅔ cup water and warm over medium heat to dissolve the sugars. Bring to a boil and cook gently and steadily until the syrup reaches 248°F on the sugar thermometer. Working quickly, remove the pan from the heat and start whisking the egg whites on medium–fast speed until stiff peaks form. Drain the softened gelatin and blot dry on a clean towel. Add to the hot syrup and combine quickly with a rubber spatula. With the mixer on slow to medium speed, pour the hot syrup onto the egg whites in a slow and steady stream, being careful not to the pour the syrup directly onto the moving whisk or it will splatter up the sides of the bowl and not mix into the egg whites. The egg whites will foam up as the hot syrup is added. Increase the speed and continue whisking for another 3–4 minutes until the mixture is thick and glossy. Add the spices and whisk for 5 seconds to combine.

Pour the marshmallow into the prepared pan and spread level. Leave to cool to room temperature, then cover with plastic wrap and leave to set for at least 4 hours or overnight until firm.

Sprinkle the reserved confectioner's sugar mix on a baking sheet. Turn the marshmallow onto the baking sheet and carefully peel off the lining paper. Cut into pieces with a greased kitchen knife, tossing each in the confectioner's sugar mix as you do so.

These marshmallows are simply delightful just as they are, but I feel that they are crying out for a large, steaming mug of hot chocolate, a comfy armchair in a cozy, quiet corner, and a good book.

Marbled Mocha Marshmallows

Makes about 40

sunflower oil, for greasing
1 tablespoon confectioner's sugar
1 tablespoon cornstarch
2 large egg whites
pinch of salt
1¾ cups superfine sugar
5 sheets platinum-grade gelatin
3–4 teaspoons coffee extract
2oz dark chocolate, coarsely grated

Equipment

8-inch square baking pan
sugar thermometer

Store

The marshmallows will keep in an airtight box between layers of nonstick parchment paper for up to 1 week.

Lightly grease the baking pan with sunflower oil, and line with nonstick parchment paper. Lightly grease the parchment. Combine the confectioner's sugar and cornstarch in a small bowl. Dust the parchment paper with a coating of the confectioner's sugar mix and tip the excess back into the bowl, and set aside.

Place the egg whites in the bowl of a free-standing mixer fitted with a whisk attachment. Add the salt and 1 tablespoon of the superfine sugar and set aside. Place the gelatin sheets in a mixing bowl, cover with cold water, and leave to soften for 10 minutes.

Add the remaining superfine sugar to a small to medium-sized saucepan and add ½ cup water. Warm over low–medium heat to dissolve the sugar. Raise the heat and cook the syrup at a steady boil until it reaches 248°F on the sugar thermometer. Now the multi-tasking starts. Begin whisking the egg whites on medium to fast speed until stiff peaks form. Drain the gelatin sheets from the water and blot dry on a clean towel. Working quickly, remove the pan from the heat, add the gelatin to the hot syrup, and mix well with a rubber spatula. With the mixer on medium speed, slowly and steadily pour the hot syrup onto the egg whites. Once all of the syrup has been added, increase the speed and continue to whisk on medium–high for another 3 minutes until the mixture has doubled in volume and is very thick and glossy. Add the coffee extract and whisk to combine.

Using a rubber spatula, gently fold half of the grated chocolate into the marshmallow (you want it to be marbled, so don't be too heavy handed here)— the chocolate will melt into the still-warm marshmallow mix as you do so. Using the spatula, scoop the mixture into the prepared pan and then, using an offset spatula, very gently spread it level so that it fills the pan. Allow to cool completely before covering in plastic wrap, then leave for about 4 hours to set completely.

Sprinkle the remaining grated chocolate and the confectioner's sugar mix on a large baking sheet. Turn the marshmallow out onto the baking sheet and carefully peel off the parchment paper. Using a hot or lightly greased kitchen knife, cut the marshmallow into squares, dusting the sides of each piece in the chocolate and confectioner's sugar mix as you do so to prevent them sticking together.

If you like, you could serve these marshmallows as a sweet fondue at the end of a meal. Simply present your guests with a large bowl of marshmallows, another of melted chocolate, and a selection of toppings, and let them get creative and messy. I have given suggestions for three toppings I like, but there is no end to the variations you could try; toasted coconut, freeze-dried banana, sugar sprinkles, salted peanuts…

Double Dipped *Marshmallows*

Makes about 30

sunflower oil, for greasing
2 tablespoons
    confectioner's sugar
2 tablespoons cornstarch
6 sheets platinum-grade
    gelatin
2 large egg whites
pinch of salt
1¾ cups superfine sugar
1 tablespoon liquid glucose
    or corn syrup
1 teaspoon vanilla bean
    paste or the seeds from
    1 vanilla pod
4oz dark chocolate,
    chopped
⅓ cup toasted pecans,
    finely chopped
1oz freeze-dried raspberries
¼ cup chocolate sprinkles

Equipment
8-inch square baking pan
sugar thermometer

Store
The marshmallows will keep for up to 1 week in an airtight container.

Lightly grease the baking pan with sunflower oil, line with nonstick parchment paper, then lightly grease the paper. Mix the confectioner's sugar and cornstarch together in a small bowl and dust the lined pan. Tip any excess back into the bowl, and set aside.

Soak the gelatin sheets in cold water for about 10 minutes until soft. Place the egg whites in the bowl of a free-standing mixer fitted with a whisk attachment. Add the salt and 1 tablespoon of the superfine sugar, but don't whisk yet.

Combine the remaining superfine sugar and the glucose (or corn syrup) in a medium-sized saucepan and add ⅔ cup water. Warm over medium heat and stir gently to dissolve the sugar. Increase the heat and bring the mixture to a boil. Continue to cook at a steady boil until the syrup reaches a temperature of 248°F on the sugar thermometer. Remove the pan from the heat.

Drain the softened gelatin from the water and blot dry on a clean towel. Whisk the egg whites until stiff peaks form. Working quickly, add the gelatin to the hot syrup and stir until completely melted. With the mixer on medium speed, add the hot syrup to the egg whites in a steady stream. Add the vanilla and continue to whisk for 3–4 minutes until the mixture is cool, white, very glossy, and stiff enough to hold a firm ribbon trail when the whisk is lifted from the bowl.

Scoop the marshmallow into the prepared pan and spread level with an offset spatula. Leave to set in a cool place for at least 2 hours, then cover with plastic wrap and leave for another 4 hours or overnight.

Sprinkle the reserved confectioner's sugar mixture onto a large baking sheet. Turn the marshmallow onto the baking sheet, peel off the lining paper, and cut into squares, using a greased kitchen knife.

Melt the chocolate in a heatproof bowl set over a pan of barely simmering water, making sure it doesn't touch the water. Stir until smooth, remove from the heat, and cool slightly. Place the toasted pecans in a shallow bowl. Grind the freeze-dried raspberries using a mortar and pestle and transfer to another bowl, then place the sprinkles in a third. Dip the bottom of each marshmallow in melted chocolate and then into one of the toppings to coat. Leave to set on parchment paper.

Fruit

Turkish Delight

Pomegranate and Blood Orange Turkish Delight

Apricot Honey Turkish Delight

Peach Pastilles

Summer Berry Pastilles

Black Currant Pastilles

Chocolate-dipped Pear Wafers

Orangettes

Fruit Roll-ups

Fig, Pistachio, and Honey Balls

When chocolate and toffees seem like too much, you need some respite from nougat and marshmallows, or maybe you are craving something more delicate—here is your salvation. Fruit. But not just fruit: Fruit as candy, of course.

Some candies remind me of certain celebrations and events. I find it impossible to think about Christmas without sugar-dusted Turkish Delight, layered between sheets of wax paper, packaged in a beautiful box and nestled somewhere on the festive table. Or neat little bags of candied Orangettes, half coated in dark chocolate and snuck into Christmas stockings.

Fruit Pastilles beautifully capture the intense fruit flavors of summer, and I think that they are best when made with berries or summer fruit, the vibrant berry colors making the candies look like a box of sugar-coated jewels.

When making any candies with fresh fruit, try to use only ripe and seasonal produce; it will taste far better than anything out of season or fruit that has been picked under-ripe and transported halfway around the world. If you are lucky enough to grow your own fruits, I can't think of a more delicious and wonderful way to make use of your delicious garden berries or plums.

Made the traditional way with cornstarch to thicken rather than gelatin, Turkish Delight will have a beautiful, soft, melt-in-the-mouth texture and delicate flavor. It makes a perfect gift when packaged in pretty boxes between layers of wax paper.

Rosewater can vary in strength from brand to brand, so add it gingerly if you're unsure—it can be overwhelming if you are heavy-handed. The same applies to food coloring!

Turkish *Delight*

Makes 50–70 pieces

sunflower oil, for greasing
¾ cup cornstarch, plus
    2 tablespoons
2 tablespoons
    confectioner's sugar
3¾ cups superfine sugar
1 teaspoon cream of tartar
1 tablespoon lemon juice
1 teaspoon rosewater
red and yellow food-
    coloring pastes
¼ cup shelled (unsalted)
    pistachios
1 teaspoon finely grated
    lemon zest or ½ teaspoon
    lemon extract

Equipment

2 x 7-inch square baking
    pans
sugar thermometer

Store

Turkish Delight will keep in a box between layers of wax paper, with the remaining sugar mix sprinkled around it, for 1 week to 10 days at cool room temperature.

Lemon Turkish Delight pictured left page 85, Rose Turkish Delight pictured top page 84.

Grease the pans with sunflower oil, line the base and sides with plastic wrap, and lightly grease the plastic wrap. In a small bowl, mix together the 2 tablespoons cornstarch and the confectioner's sugar and sift a light coating of the mixture over the plastic wrap. Tip the excess back into the bowl and set aside.

Combine the superfine sugar, half the cream of tartar, and the lemon juice in a medium-sized, heavy-bottomed saucepan (preferably a pan with one handle rather than two to make pouring easier) and add 1½ cups water. Warm over medium heat to dissolve the sugar. Pop the sugar thermometer into the pan and bring the syrup to a boil, stirring occasionally. Continue to cook steadily until the syrup reaches 257°F. Remove the pan from the heat and keep warm.

In another medium-sized pan, whisk the remaining cornstarch and cream of tartar plus 1⅔ cups water until smooth. Bring to a boil over low heat, whisking constantly. As the mixture heats it will thicken dramatically and turn from a white liquid to a very thick, translucent paste. Simmer for 15 seconds and then pour one quarter of the hot syrup into the pan in a steady stream, whisking constantly to combine the two mixtures into a totally smooth paste. Add the remaining hot syrup in three batches, whisking constantly. Bring back to a boil and continue to cook over low to medium heat for about 30 minutes until the mixture is smooth, very thick, and glossy. Stir the mixture frequently to ensure it cooks evenly without catching on the bottom of the pan. It should be the consistency of softly whipped cream and come away from the sides of the pan in a seething mass.

Take the pan off the heat and pour half of the mixture into a bowl. Add the rosewater and a tiny amount of food coloring to make a delicate rather than shocking pink Turkish Delight. Beat until smooth and thoroughly incorporated before adding the pistachios. Pour the mixture into one of the prepared pans and spread level. Add a touch of yellow food coloring and lemon zest or extract to the remaining mixture and mix to combine. Pour into the second pan, spreading level. Once completely cold, cover the pans with plastic wrap and leave overnight in a cool place to set firm.

Tip the reserved cornstarch and confectioner's sugar mixture onto a large baking sheet. Turn the Turkish Delight out of the pans onto the baking sheet and carefully peel off the plastic wrap. Using a lightly greased kitchen knife, cut into squares, dusting each piece in the cornstarch confectioner's sugar mix as you do so.

Look out for large, heavy pomegranates since these will yield the most juice. Luckily for us, pomegranates and blood oranges are in season at the same time, making them perfect partners.

Pomegranate and Blood Orange
Turkish Delight

Makes 30–40 pieces

sunflower oil, for greasing
¾ cup cornstarch, plus
   2 tablespoons
2 tablespoons
   confectioner's sugar
2 large pomegranates
2 blood oranges
3¼ cups superfine sugar
1 teaspoon cream of tartar
2 teaspoons lemon juice
⅓ cup blanched almonds,
   lightly toasted and roughly
   chopped

Equipment
7–8 inch square baking pan
sugar thermometer

Store
Turkish Delight will keep in a box between layers of wax paper, with the remaining sugar mix sprinkled around it, for 1 week to 10 days at cool room temperature.

Pictured left page 84.

Grease the pan with sunflower oil, line the base and sides with plastic wrap, and lightly grease the plastic wrap.

In a small bowl mix together the 2 tablespoons cornstarch and the confectioner's sugar and sift a light coating of the mixture over the plastic wrap. Tip the excess out of the pan and back into the bowl and set aside until needed.

Cut the pomegranates and oranges in half and squeeze the juice using an orange squeezer—they should yield 1⅔–2 cups juice. Add enough water to make the quantity up to 2½ cups. Pour half of this liquid into a medium-sized, heavy-bottomed saucepan. Add the superfine sugar, half the cream of tartar, and lemon juice. Warm the pan over medium heat to dissolve the sugar, stirring from time to time. Pop the sugar thermometer into the pan, bring to a boil, and continue to cook steadily until the syrup reaches 257°F.

Meanwhile, in another larger pan, whisk the remaining juice, ¾ cup cornstarch, and remaining cream of tartar until smooth. Place the pan over low to medium heat and, whisking constantly, bring to a boil. The mixture will change dramatically to a thick, translucent paste. Simmer for 10 seconds and then pour a quarter of the hot syrup into the pan in a steady stream, whisking quickly and constantly to combine the two mixtures into a silky smooth paste. Add the remaining hot syrup in three batches, whisking constantly as you do so. Any lumps in your mixture at this stage will be impossible to remove later.

Bring back to a boil and continue to cook over a steady low to medium heat, stirring frequently with a heatproof rubber spatula, for about 20 minutes until the mixture is smooth, very thick and glossy, and comes away from the pan in a thick, seething mass. You will need to stir the mixture almost constantly toward the end of the cooking to ensure that it cooks evenly without catching on the bottom of the pan, and it should be the consistency of choux pastry or softly whipped cream.

Take the pan off the heat, add the almonds, and pour into the prepared pan, spreading the mixture level with an offset spatula. Leave until cold, then cover with plastic wrap and leave overnight in a cool place to set firm.

Sprinkle the reserved cornstarch and confectioner's sugar mixture on a large baking sheet. Turn the Turkish Delight out of the pan onto the cornstarch mixture and carefully peel off the plastic wrap. Using a long, greased kitchen knife, cut into squares, dusting each piece in the cornstarch confectioner's sugar mix.

I have used dried apricots here, because they have an intense flavor and are easily available. Once you've made the syrup, you don't actually need the apricots any more, but rather than waste them, try stirring them into Greek yogurt with a sprinkling of granola for breakfast.

Apricot Honey *Turkish Delight*

Makes about 50 pieces

sunflower oil, for greasing
rounded ½ cup cornstarch
   plus 2 tablespoons
2 tablespoons
   confectioner's sugar
2 cups dried apricots
⅓ cup honey plus 3
   tablespoons honey
½ vanilla pod, split
2 strips lemon peel
2 cups superfine sugar
½ teaspoon cream of tartar
squeeze of lemon juice

Equipment
7-inch square baking pan
sugar thermometer

Store
Turkish Delight will keep in a box between layers of wax paper, with the remaining sugar mix sprinkled around it, for 1 week to 10 days at cool room temperature.

Pictured right page 85.

Lightly grease the baking pan with sunflower oil, line the base and sides with plastic wrap, and lightly grease the plastic wrap. Mix together the 2 tablespoons of cornstarch and the confectioner's sugar. Dust the plastic wrap with an even layer of the confectioner's sugar mix, tip any excess back into the bowl, and set aside.

Put the dried apricots in a saucepan and add 2½ cups water, the 3 tablespoons honey, vanilla pod, and lemon peel. Gently poach the apricots for about 40 minutes until very soft and tender. From time to time, press the apricots with a wooden spoon to extract as much flavor from them as possible. Remove the pan from the heat and leave to cool for at least 2 hours.

Pass through a sieve, pressing down on the apricots to extract as much juice as possible. Measure the resulting liquid (you should have about 1⅔ cups) and add enough water to bring it up to 2½ cups. Pour half into a medium saucepan, add the superfine sugar, remaining honey, half the cream of tartar, and the lemon juice. Warm over low heat to dissolve the sugar, stirring frequently. Pop the sugar thermometer into the pan and bring the syrup to a boil. Continue to boil steadily on medium heat until the syrup reaches 257°F.

In another saucepan, whisk the remaining 1¼ cups apricot liquid, cream of tartar, and ½ cup cornstarch until smooth. Place over low heat, whisking constantly until the mixture comes to a boil, thickens quite dramatically and goes from opaque to a translucent paste. Remove the pan from the heat and, whisking constantly, slowly add a quarter of the hot apricot syrup. Add the remaining syrup in three batches, whisking really well until totally smooth between each addition. (Any lumps in the mixture at this stage will be impossible to remove later.) Return the pan to low heat and, stirring frequently with a heatproof rubber spatula to prevent the sugar catching on the bottom of the pan, continue to cook for about 30 minutes, until the mixture is very thick, glossy, and smooth, and comes away from the sides of the pan in a seething mass. It should be the consistency of softly whipped cream. Taste, and add a drop of lemon juice if needed. Pour into the prepared pan and spread level with an offset spatula. Leave until cold, then cover with plastic wrap and leave overnight to set.

Sprinkle the reserved confectioner's sugar and cornstarch mixture on a large baking sheet in an even layer. Carefully turn the Turkish Delight out of the pan and onto the confectioner's sugar mixture and peel off the plastic wrap. Using a lightly oiled large kitchen knife, cut the Turkish Delight into 1-inch squares, dusting each piece with the confectioner's sugar mix as you do so to prevent them from sticking together. Store in a cardboard box in layers separated by sheets of wax paper.

When making pastilles you should seek out seasonal, ripe fruit for best results—fruit that is out of season or under-ripe will never taste as good as its sun-ripened cousins, whatever you do to it.

You could use ripe apricots or nectarines in place of peaches in this recipe and maybe add the seeds from half a vanilla pod to the mix.

Please refer to the Notes on Making Fruit Pastilles, page 88.

Peach *Pastilles*

Makes 40–50

sunflower oil, for greasing
4 large, ripe yellow-flesh
   peaches
1¾ cups superfine sugar
1–2 tablespoons lemon
   juice
½ tablespoon apple-based
   liquid pectin
¾ cup granulated sugar,
   for coating

Equipment
7-inch square baking pan
sugar thermometer

Store
Pastilles will keep for
2 weeks in an airtight
container.

Pictured page 92.

Lightly grease the baking pan and line with plastic wrap, making sure that it comes all the way up the sides.

Cut a cross through the skin on the underside of each peach, place in a bowl, cover with boiling water, and leave for 30 seconds to loosen the skin. Drain and, using a sharp knife, carefully peel off the skins. Roughly chop the peach flesh, discarding the pit. Place the peach flesh in a saucepan and add 1 tablespoon of the superfine sugar and 1 tablespoon of lemon juice. Cook the fruit over low heat for about 3–4 minutes until it has softened. Blend the peaches until smooth. Pass through a sieve and weigh the smooth puree.

Pour 14oz of the puree into a clean, medium-sized pan. Add the remaining superfine sugar and warm over low heat to dissolve the sugar, stirring frequently. Pop the sugar thermometer into the pan and bring to a gentle simmer. Continue to cook until it reaches 225°F, stirring from time to time with a heatproof rubber spatula to prevent the mixture catching on the bottom of the pan.

Add the pectin and a dash of lemon juice, whisk to combine and then continue to cook for another couple of minutes until the mixture returns to 225°F. Stir frequently to prevent it catching on the bottom of the pan; the mixture should be very thick and jamlike. To test if it has reached setting point, drop half a teaspoon of the mixture into a bowl of cold water—it should set into a soft ball. If it doesn't, continue to cook for a couple of minutes, stirring almost constantly and testing again every minute. Pour the mixture into the prepared pan and spread level. Leave in a cool place until completely cold and then cover with plastic wrap and leave overnight until firm.

The next day, spread the granulated sugar on a baking sheet in an even layer. Carefully turn the Peach Pastille out of the pan and onto the sugar, top-side down. Gently peel off the plastic wrap and, using a hot or lightly greased kitchen knife, cut into 1-inch squares, coating each piece in granulated sugar as you do so to prevent them from sticking together.

Leave the pastilles to dry for 30 minutes to 1 hour before shaking off any excess sugar and packaging into pretty boxes between layers of wax or nonstick paper.

Notes on Making Fruit Pastilles

My grandmother always seemed to have a box of Meltis New Berry Fruits when we went to visit. Packaged in a pretty box in a variety of flavors, each with a soft, fruity center, they were fancy and really meant for grown-ups only. But there wasn't a flavor that I didn't love. If you wanted to give the pastilles on the following pages the same airs and graces, you could call them by their French name of *pâtes de fruits* and pack them into pretty boxes, too.

Fruit pastilles aren't exactly tricky to make, but you will need to give them your undivided attention and be prepared for a certain amount of stirring and thermometer watching. They can take up to an hour to make, depending on the water and pectin content of your fruit puree, but don't be tempted to speed up and rush the cooking process or you could risk scorching the mixture on the bottom of the pan, thereby ruining the delicious fruit flavors.

Fruit pastilles can be made in myriad flavors and colors, but I think that berries and summer fruit work particularly well. You can use your imagination, though, and play around with what you happen to have and what's in season. Try other flavor combinations—such as adding passionfruit or rosewater to strawberries, vanilla seeds to peaches, and fresh ginger to apricots—and always use ripe, seasonal, and flavorsome fruit for the best results.

All you need is a sugar thermometer, a heavy-bottomed saucepan, a heatproof rubber spatula, and about one hour. As with most candy making, you will find that the best results are achieved by using a heavy-bottomed saucepan: Sweetened fruit puree is delicate and will almost certainly catch and burn on the bottom of a thin pan, and any burnt sugar or fruit will taint the delicate fruity flavor of your pastilles. I also find the heatproof rubber spatula is essential for stirring these mixtures as it gets into the corners of the pan that can be hard to reach with a wooden spoon.

For all of my fruit pastille recipes, I suggest using liquid pectin. This is available in many supermarkets in the baking aisle or online.

Cooking times for each recipe will vary depending on the water content and ripeness of the fruit and so should be used as a guideline rather than a strict rule.

As in most of my candy-making adventures I prefer to make pastilles in smaller batches for a number of reasons. It's quicker, for a start; I find it easier; and I make a variety of flavors at the same time.

To make double-layered pastilles, simply make two different flavors and colors that will complement each other, such as black currant and peach. Set each flavor into separate large baking sheets lined with plastic wrap and leave for a couple of hours until firm, but still slightly soft and sticky to touch. Cut each flavor into three rectangles. Carefully flip one rectangle of one flavor on top of the surface of another contrasting flavor and press gently together. Cover and leave overnight until firm, before cutting into shapes and coating in granulated sugar.

If you are of the romantic persuasion, rather than cutting these pastilles into small disks or squares, you could cut them into heart shapes using a small cookie cutter. Keep any scraps as a treat for yourself in an airtight container and don't tell anyone about them—it can be our secret.

Please refer to the Notes on Making Fruit Pastilles, page 88.

Summer Berry *Pastilles*

Makes 40–50

sunflower oil, for greasing
1lb mixed strawberries
    and raspberries
2 tablespoons lemon juice
2 cups superfine sugar
2 tablespoons apple-based
    liquid pectin
¾ cup granulated sugar

Equipment
7–8 inch square baking pan
sugar thermometer
heart-shaped or small round
    cookie cutter (optional)

Store
Pastilles will keep for
2 weeks in an airtight
container.

Lightly grease the baking pan and line with plastic wrap, making sure that it comes all the way up the sides.

Hull and quarter the strawberries. Tip them into a pan with the raspberries, 1 tablespoon of the lemon juice, and 2 tablespoons of the superfine sugar. Cook gently until the berries are soft and juicy. Push though a fine mesh sieve to remove the seeds and weigh the resulting puree.

Pour 14oz of puree into a clean pan, add the remaining superfine sugar, and warm over low heat, stirring frequently, until the sugar has dissolved. Pop the sugar thermometer into the pan and bring to a boil. Continue to cook slowly and steadily until the mixture reaches 225°F, stirring frequently to prevent the mixture from scorching on the bottom of the pan.

Add the remaining lemon juice and the pectin to the pan and whisk to combine. Continue to cook, stirring frequently, until the puree returns to 225°F and is very thick and almost jamlike. To test if it has reached setting point, drop half a teaspoon of mixture into a bowl of cold water— it should set into a soft ball. If not, continue to cook for a couple of minutes, stirring constantly and testing every minute.

Pour the mixture into the pan in an even layer and leave until cold. Cover with plastic wrap and leave overnight until set firm.

The next day, spread the granulated sugar on a baking sheet in an even layer and carefully flip the Summer Berry Pastille onto the sugar. Peel off the plastic wrap and, using a hot or lightly greased kitchen knife, cut the pastille into ½-inch squares (or hearts and circles, using lightly greased cutters). Coat each piece in granulated sugar and leave to dry for 30 minutes to 1 hour before shaking off any excess and packing the pastilles into boxes between layers of wax or nonstick parchment paper.

When I was little, black currant pastilles were my all-time favorite flavor and would always be the first to go from the box. Black currants have a short season so it's worth buying lots when available and keeping a stash of either fruit or puree in the freezer; that way, you can indulge in some pastille making whenever you feel the urge.

Black currants are naturally high in pectin, which means that this mixture thickens faster than others, so keep an eye on it as it cooks and don't get sidetracked by other business.

Please refer to the Notes on Making Fruit Pastilles, page 88.

Black Currant *Pastilles*

Makes about 40

sunflower oil, for greasing
14oz black currants or
    blackberries
around 2 cups superfine
    sugar
2 tablespoons lemon juice
1 tablespoon apple-based
    liquid pectin
¾ cup granulated sugar

Equipment
7–8 inch square baking pan
sugar thermometer

Store
Pastilles will keep for up
to 2 weeks in an airtight
container in a cool place.

Lightly grease the baking pan and line with plastic wrap, making sure that it comes all the way up the sides.

Remove any stems from the black currants and tip the fruit into a pan. Add 1 tablespoon of the superfine sugar and 1 tablespoon of lemon juice and cook gently until the fruit is soft and juicy. Tip into a fine mesh sieve set over a bowl and push the fruit through to make a smooth puree.

Weigh the puree and pour 10oz into a clean, heavy-bottomed pan with 1¾ cups of the remaining sugar. Warm over low heat, stirring frequently, to dissolve the sugar. Pop the sugar thermometer into the pan and cook slowly and steadily until the mixture reaches 225°F. You will need to stir frequently to prevent the mixture from catching on the bottom of the pan. Carefully taste (it will be hot) and add a little more sugar if your black currants are especially tart. Add another tablespoon of lemon juice and the pectin, mix to thoroughly combine, and continue to cook, stirring frequently with a heatproof rubber spatula, until the mixture thickens to the consistency of soft jam and returns to 225°F.

To test if the mixture will set, drop half a teaspoon into a bowl of cold water and it should form into a ball. If not, continue to cook for a couple of minutes, stirring constantly and testing every minute.

Pour into the prepared pan in an even layer and leave until completely cold before covering with plastic wrap. Leave overnight to set firm.

The next day, spread the granulated sugar on a baking sheet. Turn the pastille mixture onto the sugar, carefully peeling off the plastic wrap lining, and use a hot or lightly greased kitchen knife to cut into small squares. Toss each piece in sugar to coat and to prevent them sticking together.

Leave the pastilles to dry for 30 minutes to 1 hour. Shake off the excess sugar and serve, or pack into boxes between layers of wax paper or nonstick parchment paper.

Some chocolates are meant to be packaged into pretty boxes, savored and nibbled one piece at a time, while others are meant to be made and eaten as soon as possible. These elegant wafers sit firmly in the consume-soon-after-making camp. I like to serve them with a small glass of something sweet, sticky, and alcoholic after a good, rich dinner.

It's tricky to slice pears thinly and evenly using a knife, and the results will be more elegant using a mandolin, so if you have one, I suggest you dust it off for this recipe. Any leftover or uneven pear slices can be baked into a cake, tossed into a salad, or made into Fruit Roll-ups (see page 98).

Chocolate-dipped *Pear Wafers*

Makes about 30

¼ cup superfine sugar
juice of ½ lemon
½ teaspoon vanilla bean
  paste or seeds from
  ½ vanilla pod
3 firm pears
5oz dark chocolate, finely
  chopped

Equipment
mandolin
2 baking sheets

Store
I would suggest eating these wafers on the day you make them.

Preheat the oven to 225°F.

Put the sugar, lemon juice, vanilla paste or seeds, and ⅓ cup water in a small pan and bring to a boil. Simmer for 2 minutes, then remove from the heat.

Using a mandolin, slice the pears vertically (i.e. through the stem) into thin slices. Dip each slice into the syrup, so that it coats both sides, allowing any excess to drip back into the pan. Lay the slices in a single layer on parchment paper-lined baking sheets. Bake on the middle and lower shelves of the oven for about 2 hours, turning the slices on the parchment and swapping the sheets after 1 hour. When the pears are beginning to crisp and are pale golden in color, remove from the oven and transfer to a cooling rack. The pears will crisp more as they cool; once they are completely cold they are ready for dipping.

Melt the chocolate in a heatproof bowl set over a pan of barely simmering water., making sure the bottom of the bowl doesn't touch the water. Stir until smooth and leave to cool slightly.

Taking one pear wafer at a time, dip the less attractive side into the melted chocolate to coat evenly, then place on a parchment-lined baking sheet, chocolate side down. Repeat with the remaining pears. Leave until the chocolate has hardened before serving.

I always think of Orangettes as "man chocolates"—partly due to the fact that they are a particular favorite of my stepfather, and his Christmas stocking is incomplete without a package of these tucked in among the brightly colored socks and a good book.

These candied orange peels are tickled with a hint of spice in the syrup, making them a little more special; feel free to play around with flavors here—you could try adding a little ginger to the mix if you prefer.

rangettes

Makes 50–60

3 oranges
1¾ cups superfine sugar
1 star anise
½ vanilla pod
6 cardamom pods, bruised
1 cinnamon stick
½ teaspoon pink
   peppercorns
7oz dark chocolate,
   chopped
finely chopped pistachios or
   edible gold leaf (optional)

Store
Orangettes—either coated or
not—will keep in an airtight
container or jar out of direct
sunlight for 2–3 weeks.

Take a small, sharp kitchen knife and cut through the skin of each orange; you want to just cut through the skin to the flesh and mark each orange into quarters. Carefully peel the skin away from the orange in neat quarters and slice into strips ½ inch wide. Save the orange flesh for use in another recipe or simply eat as it is and boost your vitamin C intake.

Place the sliced peels in a saucepan, cover with cold water, and bring to a boil. Simmer for 2 minutes and then drain. Repeat this process twice more (this softens the orange skin and removes any lingering bitterness), then drain the peels and set aside while you prepare the syrup.

Tip the sugar into a heavy-bottomed pan and add 1½ cups water. Pop the star anise, vanilla and cardamom pods, cinnamon stick, and peppercorns into the pan and warm over medium heat to gently dissolve the sugar, stirring from time to time. Add the peels to the pan and boil slowly and steadily for about 40 minutes, stirring occasionally, until the peels become soft and translucent and almost all of the syrup has been absorbed. Keep a close eye on the pan for the last 10 minutes because the syrup becomes very thick and can easily burn.

Using tongs, remove the peels from the pan one at a time, and lay on a sheet of parchment paper in a single layer, leaving space between each piece. Leave the Orangettes on the paper to dry overnight. Once they are candied and no longer sticky, store in an airtight container between layers of wax paper.

Melt the chocolate in a heatproof bowl set over a pan of barely simmering water, making sure the bottom of the bowl doesn't touch the water. Stir until smooth, remove from the heat, and cool slightly. Dip one end of each Orangette into the melted chocolate, sprinkle with pistachios (if using), and leave to dry on parchment paper. Once the chocolate has set, add a tickle of edible gold leaf.

Fruit *Roll-ups*

Not only are these super-scrumptious, but they are also a great way to use up fruit that is idling in the fruit bowl. I find that apples or pears provide a good base to which you can add other fruits such as berries, peaches, plums, apricots, or mangoes. I prefer not to oversweeten the puree to allow the flavors of the fruit to really shine through. Each variation makes about 4–6 roll-ups, depending on how large you cut them.

Apple and Pear

2 ripe pears, peeled, cored, and chopped
2 apples, peeled, cored, and chopped
juice of ½ lemon
1–2 tablespoons agave syrup or honey

Equipment
10 x 16 inch jelly roll pan

Store
Roll-ups will keep for up to 1 month in an airtight container or jar.

Preheat the oven to 225°F. Line the pan with nonstick parchment paper.

Puree the fruit in a blender. Add the lemon juice and agave syrup or honey and blend until you have a silky smooth puree. Tip into a saucepan and cook very gently, stirring from time to time, until reduced by half and thickened to a loose jam consistency. Taste and add a little more agave or honey if you think it's needed. Spoon the mixture onto the parchment paper and use an offset spatula to spread thinly and evenly.

Cook the fruit on the middle shelf of the oven for about 3 hours until the fruit is no longer sticky and will start to peel off the paper. Turn the pan around halfway through to ensure that the mixture cooks evenly. Remove from the oven and leave to cool, before carefully peeling off the parchment paper and cutting the fruit leather into strips, around 2 inches wide. Lay each strip on a similar-sized strip of nonstick parchment paper, roll up into a tight coil, and secure with tape or kitchen twine.

Apple and Berry

2 apples, peeled, cored, and chopped
2 cups blackberries or blueberries
1 tablespoon lemon juice
1–2 tablespoons agave syrup or clear honey

Preheat the oven to 225°F. Line the pan with nonstick parchment paper. Cut the apples into chunks and blend with the blackberries, lemon juice, and agave syrup or honey until smooth. Pass the puree through a sieve into a saucepan to remove the berry seeds. Cook gently until reduced by half and thickened to a loose jam consistency. Remove the pan from the heat and spread the puree on to the prepared jelly roll pan in an even layer using an offset spatula. Cook as above.

Strawberry and Pear

2 cups ripe strawberries (or mixture of strawberries and raspberries)
2 ripe pears, peeled and cored
1 tablespoon lemon juice
1–2 tablespoons agave syrup or honey

Preheat the oven to 225°F. Line the pan with nonstick parchment paper.

Hull and halve the strawberries, chop the pears, and blend to a smooth puree together with the lemon juice and agave syrup or honey. Scoop the puree into a saucepan and continue as above.

If you were in the market for something a little healthier than a chocolate truffle, salted caramel, or nougat bar, then you have come to the right place. And while they may well be healthier, these fruit-and-nut-packed treats are no less yummy. While not promising great wealth, happiness, or supermodel good looks, they will make you feel a smidgeon less guilty about indulging in something sweet. Sneak them into lunchboxes or serve after dinner with fresh mint tea.

Fig, Pistachio, and Honey Balls

Makes about 20–25

¾ cup shelled, unsalted
  pistachios
⅓ cup blanched almonds
4 Medjool dates
1⅓ cups dried figs
1–2 teaspoons finely grated
  orange zest
1–2 teaspoons orange-
  flower water or rosewater
2 tablespoons honey
½ teaspoon ground
  cinnamon
cocoa for dusting (optional)

Store
These will keep for up to
2 weeks in an airtight
container in the fridge.

Grind the pistachios and almonds in a food processor using the pulse button (or by hand with a kitchen knife) until finely chopped but not powdery. Tip into a bowl. Remove the pits from the dates and cut the tough stem ends from the figs. Very roughly chop the dried fruit and then process until almost smooth in the food processor. Add the orange zest, orange-flower water or rosewater, honey, and cinnamon and briefly process again until just combined. Tip into the bowl with the chopped nuts and mix until thoroughly combined.

Using your hands, roll the mixture into cherry-sized balls and place on a parchment-covered baking sheet. Cover and chill until firm.

Just before serving, lightly dust the balls in cocoa if desired.

Toffee, Fudge, and Caramels

Bonfire Toffee

Vanilla and Chocolate Swirls

Chocolate and Ginger Fudge

Vanilla Fudge

Cherry Brandy Fudge

Maple Pecan Fudge

Coffee and Toasted Almond Fudge

Goat Milk and Vanilla Bean Caramels

Buttered Salted Caramels

Coconut Milk Caramels

Double Chocolate Caramels

This chapter should be subtitled "Hot Sugar," because this is exactly what all of the following recipes have in common. There are many things that I love about candy making, but it's the umpteen ways to use certain everyday ingredients, and in particular sugar, that excite me most. This is kitchen alchemy at its best and most fascinating. The variety of delicious things that can be made from a few simple ingredients, cooked using slightly different techniques and at slightly different temperatures, is nothing short of wondrous. Sugar, cream, a drop of vanilla, a pat of butter, and a few other delights, and you can make soft creamy fudge, snappy dark toffees, and chewy caramel.

I don't think I know anyone who can resist buttery salted caramels or a square of creamy, vanilla-flecked fudge, and the sweet aroma of a pan of caramel gently bubbling away on the stove is surely a smell to rival that of freshly baked bread.

As a junior cook I would spend hours in my mother's kitchen in a pursuit of perfect fudge. My mother is a very understanding and patient woman, and she encouraged every attempt, but after numerous pans of burnt sugar, too crumbly or too-soft-to-set fudge, we learned the hard way that the one vital thing missing was a sugar thermometer. Now, I would not even consider making any Hot Sugar recipe without my trusty thermometer by my side (or in my pan).

One word of warning—boiling hot sugar can be dangerous, so please exercise caution when you are around pans of bubbling caramel, fudge, or toffee.

Bonfire Toffee reminds me of my grandfather, who was very fond of a particular brand of toffees. On holidays he would receive a gift box and would happily share the toffees with anyone who happened to be passing. We kids would always choose the pale creamy toffees, leaving him with the darker ones, but he didn't seem to mind at all. And now I know why—molasses gives toffee a deep, dark, slightly smoky taste that's altogether more worldly wise and mysterious than its creamy counterpart.

Bonfire Toffee

Makes about 50 squares

sunflower oil, for greasing
5oz unsalted butter, diced
1 cup superfine sugar
½ cup molasses
6 tablespoons corn syrup
¼ cup crème fraîche
¼ teaspoon cream of tartar
pinch of sea salt flakes

Equipment
8-inch square baking pan
sugar thermometer

Store
The toffee can be stored in boxes for up to 2 weeks between layers of nonstick parchment paper or wax paper.

Grease the base and sides of the baking pan with sunflower oil and line with nonstick parchment paper.

Combine the butter, superfine sugar, molasses, corn syrup, crème fraîche, and cream of tartar in a large, heavy-bottomed saucepan with a capacity of 2½ quarts. Add the sea salt flakes and ½ cup water and warm over low to medium heat to melt the butter and dissolve the sugar, stirring from time to time.

Once the mixture is smooth and silky, pop the sugar thermometer into the pan and bring the mixture to a boil, then continue to cook steadily for about 20 minutes until the mixture reaches a temperature of 266°F.

Remove from the heat and plunge the base of the pan into a sink of cold water to slow down the cooking process. Stir the mixture a couple of times, then pour into the prepared pan and spread level.

If you like your toffee in uniform squares, try using a dough/bench scraper or knife to mark the toffee while it is still slightly warm. It will then easily cut into neat pieces once it's completely cold and hardened. Otherwise, simply leave in a cool place until firm and completely cold before breaking into chunks or squares. I like the thrill of smashing this toffee into shards of deliciousness—if you happen to have a little toffee hammer, so much the better, but if not, the end of a rolling pin works just as well—though possibly not quite as elegantly.

Here you have the best of both worlds in one indulgent mouthful. Vanilla and chocolate, rolled together into a pretty, rather fancy package. Please don't be tempted to cook either of the mixtures at lower or higher temperature than I suggest, or you'll find it practically impossible to roll them. The trick is to roll the toffee when it will peel off the paper and before it hardens too much.

Vanilla and Chocolate *Swirls*

Makes about 50

For the vanilla layer
sunflower oil, for greasing
¾ cup superfine sugar
½ cup brown sugar
5 tablespoons corn syrup
3oz unsalted butter
¾ cup heavy cream plus
   1 tablespoon
½ teaspoon vanilla bean
   paste
pinch of sea salt flakes

For the chocolate layer
2oz dark chocolate,
   chopped
2½ tablespoons unsalted
   butter
⅓ cup superfine sugar
¼ cup brown sugar
2½ tablespoons corn syrup
⅓ cup heavy cream plus
   2 tablespoons
¼ teaspoon vanilla bean
   paste
pinch of sea salt flakes

Equipment
9 x 12 inch Swiss roll pan
sugar thermometer

Store
These Swirls will keep for about 2 weeks in an airtight container in a cool place.

Lightly grease the pan with sunflower oil and line with lightly greased nonstick parchment paper.

Make the vanilla layer first. Pour the superfine sugar into a medium-sized, heavy-bottomed saucepan and add 2 tablespoons water. Set over low heat to gently dissolve the sugar, and use a pastry brush dipped in hot water to dissolve any sugar crystals that form on the sides of the pan. Meanwhile, measure the remaining ingredients into another saucepan and heat gently to melt the butter and dissolve the sugar. Bring to a boil, stir until smooth, and remove from the heat.

Once the superfine sugar has completely dissolved, increase the heat slightly and bring the syrup to a boil. Continue to cook until it turns honey-colored—watch it like a hawk, as this will only take 2–3 minutes over medium heat. Remove the pan from the heat and, very carefully, add the hot cream mixture. The caramel will hiss and splutter, so exercise caution and add the cream slowly and steadily. Stir until smooth, pop the sugar thermometer into the pan, and return to medium heat. Continue to cook over a steady, even heat until the toffee reaches 250°F on the sugar thermometer, stirring from time to time to prevent it from catching on the bottom of the pan. Give it a quick stir, then pour it into the prepared pan and spread level using an offset spatula. Leave to cool for 15 minutes and then prepare the chocolate layer.

Combine all the chocolate layer ingredients into a small, heavy-bottomed saucepan and set over low heat to melt the chocolate and butter and dissolve the sugars. Once the mixture is silky smooth, pop the sugar thermometer into the pan and bring to a boil over medium heat. Continue to cook until it reaches 239°F. Remove the pan from the heat, stir briefly, and pour the chocolate mixture evenly over the vanilla layer, spreading it level using an offset spatula. Leave to cool for about an hour until cold and firm but not solid. It is ready to roll if you can slide an offset spatula between the toffee and the parchment paper.

Using a greased or warmed kitchen knife, trim the edges of the toffee on all sides and then slice in half to make two rectangles, each measuring roughly 6 x 8 inches, cutting through the parchment paper as you do so. Starting at one of the 8-inch sides, roll the end over neatly and tightly and continue to roll into a spiral log, pulling the toffee as you go. Wrap it tightly in a clean piece of parchment paper, gently rolling it on the work surface to neaten and tighten as you do so. Twist the ends of the paper to seal. Repeat with the second piece. Leave the wrapped logs to firm up for at least 4 hours or overnight before slicing into ½-inch pieces. Wrap each swirl either in nonstick parchment, wax paper, or plastic.

Like all fudges, this starts life as a light, creamy-colored mixture, then as it cooks and reduces it becomes a rich caramel color, filling the kitchen with a sweet, creamy and distinctly fudgy aroma.

Ordinarily, I like to use a good-quality chocolate with a medium-high cocoa content for my candy making—somewhere around the 64 percent mark; but for this recipe you'll need to use something a little richer—I'd go for 70 percent for a real chocolate hit. Pictured on page 111.

Chocolate and Ginger *Fudge*

Makes around 50 pieces

sunflower oil, for greasing
2½ cups superfine sugar
¾ cup evaporated milk
½ cup whole milk
⅓ cup heavy cream
pinch of sea salt
4oz dark chocolate
3oz preserved ginger in
   syrup, drained
2oz unsalted butter
2 teaspoons cocoa
1 teaspoon vanilla extract
   or ½ teaspoon
   vanilla bean paste

Equipment
7-inch square baking pan
sugar thermometer

Store
Store the fudge in between layers of wax or nonstick paper in an airtight container for up to 2 weeks.

Grease the pan with sunflower oil and line with nonstick baking paper.

Combine the sugar, evaporated milk, whole milk, heavy cream, and salt in a large (at least 2½-quart) heavy-bottomed saucepan and place over low to medium heat to dissolve the sugar. Once the mixture is smooth, pop the sugar thermometer into the pan and bring to a boil. The mixture will initially rise up quite alarmingly as it boils—hence the need for a large pan. Lower the heat and continue to cook over low heat, stirring frequently with a heatproof rubber spatula, until the fudge reaches 233°F on the sugar thermometer.

While the fudge mixture is cooking, chop the chocolate, finely chop the ginger, dice the butter, and sift the cocoa.

Remove the pan from the heat and add the vanilla, chocolate, ginger, butter, and cocoa and stir gently to combine. Spoon the fudge into a bowl and set aside to cool for 3 minutes. Beat the cooled fudge with a rubber spatula or wooden spoon until it thickens and starts to lose its glossy sheen (this will take less time than regular fudge—about 1 minute). Spoon into the prepared pan, spread level, and leave until completely cold and firm before cutting into pieces to serve.

My mother and I normally like the same things—we both have a sweet tooth and I blame her for my love of candies and chocolate. However, when it comes to fudge, I err on the side of creamy while my mum likes fudge with a little more texture, a little more grit. So this one is for her. Pictured on page 111.

Vanilla Fudge

Makes about 50 pieces

sunflower oil, for greasing
14oz can condensed milk
⅔ cup whole milk
1 cup brown sugar
1 cup superfine sugar
pinch of sea salt flakes
4oz unsalted butter
1 teaspoon vanilla bean
  paste

Equipment
8-inch square baking pan
sugar thermometer

Store
This fudge will keep for about 2 weeks in an airtight container between layers of nonstick parchment paper or wax paper.

Grease the baking pan with sunflower oil and line with nonstick baking paper.

Combine all of the ingredients apart from the butter and vanilla in a 2½-quart saucepan and place over low heat to dissolve the sugars, stirring frequently. Once the mixture is smooth, raise the heat slightly and bring to a boil, again stirring to prevent the mixture from catching and scorching on the bottom of the pan. Pop the sugar thermometer into the pan, reduce the heat to a gentle simmer, and continue to cook until the mixture reaches 237–240°F. Continue to stir the fudge frequently as it cooks.

Remove the pan from the heat as soon as the fudge reaches the required temperature. Pour the fudge into a large mixing bowl, add the butter and vanilla paste, stir once or twice to combine, and leave to cool for 5–7 minutes without stirring.

Using a rubber spatula or wooden spoon, beat the fudge until it thickens, loses its shine, and starts to become grainy. Pour into the prepared pan, spread level, and leave until completely cold before cutting into pieces to serve.

Although delicious, the classic combination of rum and raisin seems to me a little dated and reminiscent of the 1970s, and so here I've given the dried-fruit-and-alcohol double act a modern twist, bathing dried soft cherries, which I love, in cherry brandy and vanilla. However, if you prefer, just use the same quantity of raisins and soak them in rum.

Cherry Brandy *Fudge*

Makes about 50 pieces

sunflower oil, for greasing
⅔ cup dried cherries
3–4 tablespoons cherry
   brandy
½ vanilla pod
2¼ cups superfine sugar
2½ tablespoons corn syrup
2 tablespoons liquid glucose
¾ cup evaporated milk
¾ cup whole milk
2oz unsalted butter
pinch of salt

Equipment

7-inch square baking pan
sugar thermometer

Store

This fudge will keep for about 2 weeks in an airtight container in between layers of wax or nonstick parchment paper.

Grease the base and sides of the baking pan with sunflower oil and line with a sheet of nonstick parchment paper.

Place the cherries in a small saucepan and add the cherry brandy. Cut the vanilla pod to expose the seeds and add it to the cherries. Set the pan over low heat for about 3 minutes to warm the brandy but don't allow it to boil. Remove from the heat and leave to cool, stirring occasionally, so that the cherries soak up all of the vanilla-infused brandy.

Half-fill the sink with cold water.

To make the fudge, combine the remaining ingredients and the brandied vanilla pod in a large saucepan (ideally one with a capacity of around 2½ quarts) and set the pan over low heat to melt the butter and dissolve the sugar.

Pop the sugar thermometer into the pan and raise the heat to bring the mixture to a boil—at this stage, it will be a deep creamy color, but as it reaches the required temperature, it will turn a rich caramel color. Stirring frequently, continue to cook on steady low to medium heat until the fudge registers 237°F on the sugar thermometer. Remove the pan from the heat and plunge the base into the sink of cold water for 20 seconds to arrest the cooking.

Using tongs or a fork, remove the vanilla pod from the pan and leave the fudge to cool on a heatproof surface for 3–4 minutes; it will start to lose its surface sheen as it cools. Beat the cooled fudge with a rubber spatula for about 3 minutes until it thickens and starts to become grainy. Add the brandied cherries, mix to combine, and spoon into the prepared pan in an even layer. Leave to cool completely and then cover with plastic wrap and leave overnight before cutting into squares to serve.

I love the slightly smoky, butterscotch taste that maple syrup brings to this rather indulgent fudge, elevating it to new heights of deliciousness. I've also taken the liberty of adding a splash of bourbon to this recipe, which I think makes it even more scrumptious. I prefer fudge to be on the creamy side, but if you are of the grainy persuasion, you may need to work a little harder, and for a little longer, when it comes to beating the cooled fudge to achieve the desired texture.

This recipe makes enough fudge to fill two gift boxes—assuming, of course, that you are not planning on eating it all yourself.

Maple Pecan *Fudge*

Makes about 40 pieces

sunflower oil, for greasing
¾ cup superfine sugar
1 cup maple syrup
2 tablespoons corn syrup
⅔ cup heavy cream
⅓ cup whole milk
2 tablespoons bourbon or
   Jack Daniels
1 teaspoon vanilla extract
½ teaspoon sea salt
1oz unsalted butter
1 cup pecans, toasted and
   roughly chopped

Equipment
7-inch square baking pan
sugar thermometer

Store
This fudge will keep for up to 2 weeks in an airtight container between layers of nonstick parchment paper or wax paper.

Grease the base and sides of the pan with sunflower oil and line with nonstick parchment paper, and half fill the sink with cold water.

Combine all the ingredients apart from the butter and pecans in a large (2½ quart), heavy-bottomed saucepan. Cook gently over medium heat to dissolve the sugar, stirring frequently.

Pop the sugar thermometer into the pan, bring to a boil, and continue to steadily cook the syrup at a gentle boil until it reaches 237°F. You will need to stir the mixture frequently to prevent it catching on the bottom of the pan. (The syrup will take about 15 minutes to reach the correct temperature, but do not be tempted to walk away from the task in hand—the moment you turn your back to do something else, the syrup will go over the correct temperature and you'll end up with toffee rather than fudge.)

Take the pan off the heat, remove the sugar thermometer, and plunge the bottom of the pan into the sink of cold water to stop the mixture from cooking any more. Add the butter, give the fudge a gentle stir, and scoop it into a large mixing bowl. Leave undisturbed to cool to room temperature for about 15–20 minutes, without being tempted to stir or taste the cooling fudge.

Using a wooden spoon or rubber spatula, beat the fudge for 3–4 minutes until the mixture thickens, starts to lose its shine, and begins to turn slightly grainy. Add three-quarters of the chopped pecans and spoon the fudge into the prepared pan, spreading it into an even layer with an offset spatula. Scatter the remaining pecans over the top, pressing them into the fudge.

Leave to cool completely, then cover with plastic wrap and leave overnight before cutting into squares to serve.

I love this rich fudge, with its slightly burnt toffee flavor and distinct coffee hit. If you can get your hands on some good-quality coffee extract, you could use that in place of instant espresso powder. Extracts vary in intensity from brand to brand, so build up the flavor gradually until you reach the required flavor. The small amount of chocolate in this fudge is there just to give the coffee a little extra oomph rather than to make a full-on chocolate statement.

Coffee and Toasted Almond *Fudge*

Makes about 50 pieces

sunflower oil, for greasing
2 cups superfine sugar
½ cup brown sugar
4 tablespoons corn syrup
¾ cup evaporated milk
¾ cup whole milk
1 cinnamon stick
pinch of salt
3–4 teaspoons instant espresso powder
1oz dark chocolate
2oz unsalted butter
½ cup chopped blanched almonds, toasted

Equipment
7-inch square baking pan
sugar thermometer

Store
This fudge will keep for about 1 week in an airtight container in between layers of wax paper or nonstick parchment paper.

Grease the pan with sunflower oil and line with nonstick parchment paper.

Place both the sugars, the corn syrup, evaporated milk, whole milk, cinnamon stick, and salt in a medium-sized saucepan. Cook over low heat to dissolve the sugar, stir until smooth, and bring to just below boiling point.

Pop the sugar thermometer into the pan and bring to a boil. Cook the mixture gently and steadily, stirring from time to time with a heatproof rubber spatula, until it reaches 237°F on the sugar thermometer. Remove the cinnamon stick using either a pair of tongs or a fork.

Meanwhile, dissolve the espresso powder in 1–2 teaspoons boiling water, finely chop the chocolate, and dice the butter. Add these to the hot fudge mixture, stir until smooth, and return the pan to the heat. Bring the fudge back to 233–237°F and then immediately remove from the heat and pour into a large mixing bowl. Leave the fudge, undisturbed, to cool for 5 minutes.

Using a rubber spatula or wooden spoon, beat the fudge until it thickens and loses its glossy sheen. Add the almonds and stir to combine. Spoon into the prepared pan and spread level with an offset spatula. Leave to cool completely and then cover with plastic wrap and leave overnight before cutting into squares to serve.

Having come across a jar of goat milk and vanilla caramel sauce in a gourmet food store in Brooklyn, New York, I became fixated on recreating the idea—but in candy form. Goat milk can have quite a defined taste but it's one that softens into a delicious creaminess once reduced; I think that you'll be pleasantly surprised if you've never tried it before. I like to ask people to guess the secret ingredient in these caramels, and no one yet has guessed correctly, but everyone loves the flavor. In Mexico, goat milk is used to make *cajeta*, a rich caramel sauce not dissimilar to the Argentine dulce de leche (which is made with cow's milk).

Goat Milk and Vanilla Bean *Caramels*

Makes about 40

sunflower oil, for greasing
2 cups full-fat goat
  milk
¼ teaspoon baking soda
1¼ cups superfine sugar
½ cup brown sugar
5 tablespoons corn syrup
2oz unsalted butter
seeds from ½ vanilla pod
  or 1 teaspoon vanilla
  bean paste
½ teaspoon sea salt flakes

Equipment
7-inch square baking pan
sugar thermometer

Store
Store the caramels in an airtight container in a cool place for about 1 week.

Grease the baking pan with sunflower oil and line the base and sides with nonstick parchment paper.

Pour the goat milk into a 2-quart heavy-bottomed saucepan, add the baking soda, and whisk to combine. Set the pan over a medium heat and bring to a boil, then reduce the heat to a simmer and continue to cook gently until the milk has reduced to 1¼–1½ cups (this can take up to 30 minutes). The milk will foam up as it boils, so keep an eye on the pan and remove it from the heat and stir it with a whisk to reduce the temperature and then continue. Once reduced, the milk will turn from white to a very pale, milky-tea color. Pour the milk into a pitcher and wash the pan.

Return the reduced milk to the clean pan and add the remaining ingredients apart from the salt. Stir until the sugar has dissolved, the butter has melted, and the mixture is silky smooth. Pop the sugar thermometer into the pan and bring to a boil. Continue to cook over steady, medium heat, stirring with a heatproof rubber spatula from time to time, until the mixture reaches 250°F. It can feel like the mixture will never get above 239°F, but don't get impatient and walk away from the pan—caramel has a habit of surging up in temperature when you're not looking.

Remove the pan from the heat and take out the vanilla pod, if used, with either tongs or a fork (not your fingers). Add the salt and stir briefly with a rubber spatula or wooden spoon to combine. Pour the caramel into the prepared pan and leave to cool for at least 4 hours.

Using a hot, clean knife, cut the caramel into bite-sized pieces and wrap each one in either nonstick parchment paper or cellophane.

This delicious caramel is the starting point for a whole world of adventures. It is scrumptious as it is—cut into squares and wrapped in paper or cellophane—but I would highly recommend that you seek out some smoked sea salt flakes and try adding those for a taste sensation. You could also coat each caramel square in dark or milk chocolate. Or slice the caramel into delicate fingers and dip the undersides in melted chocolate and nuts or coconut. . .

Buttered Salted Caramels

Makes about 40

sunflower oil, for greasing
⅔ cup brown sugar
6 tablespoons corn syrup
4oz unsalted butter, diced
1 cup heavy cream
¾ cup superfine sugar
½ teaspoon sea salt flakes
  or smoked sea salt
½ teaspoon vanilla bean
  paste

Equipment
7-inch square baking pan
sugar thermometer

Store
Wrap the caramels in cellophane or parchment paper and store in an airtight container or storage jar for up to 2 weeks.

Grease the base and sides of the baking pan with sunflower oil and line with nonstick parchment paper.

Place the brown sugar, corn syrup, butter, and heavy cream in a small saucepan and gently melt the butter and dissolve the sugar. Stir until smooth, and once the mixture is hot, remove the pan from the heat.

Place the superfine sugar in a 2-quart saucepan with 2 tablespoons water and set over low heat to dissolve the sugar. Do not stir the syrup, but gently swirl the pan to ensure that the sugar dissolves evenly; use a pastry brush dipped in hot water to dissolve any sugar crystals that form on the sides of the pan. Bring the syrup to a boil and continue to cook steadily until it turns an amber color, swirling the caramel in the pan to color evenly.

Remove the pan from the heat and carefully pour the hot cream mixture into the caramel. It will hiss and splutter as you do this, so exercise caution. Stir until smooth and return the pan to medium heat. Pop the sugar thermometer into the pan and continue to cook over low to medium steady heat until the caramel reaches 250°F. Working quickly, remove the pan from the heat, add the salt flakes and vanilla, and stir briefly to combine. Pour the hot caramel into the prepared pan and leave until completely cold and firm (at least 4 hours or overnight) before cutting into pieces with either a hot or lightly greased kitchen knife.

By now, you should know that I like to give you options whenever possible, and this recipe is no exception. First up—if you want to make these caramels vegan, simply leave out the butter. Second—once you've cut the caramel into fingers, you could try dipping the underside of each caramel in melted chocolate then leave to dry on parchment paper before serving.

One word. Wow.

Coconut Milk Caramels

Makes about 40

sunflower oil, for greasing
1⅔ cups full-fat coconut milk
4-inch piece fresh ginger, peeled and thinly sliced
6 cardamon pods, bruised
2 star anise
1 large cinnamon stick
⅔ cup brown sugar
4 tablespoons corn syrup
2oz unsalted butter
1 teaspoon vanilla extract
pinch of salt
1 rounded cup superfine sugar
2 tablespoons unsweetened shredded coconut
2oz chocolate (optional) – I like to use a mixture of half milk and half dark

Equipment
7-inch square baking pan
sugar thermometer

Store
Caramels are best eaten within 1 week, but will keep for a little longer in an airtight container.

Grease the base and sides of the baking pan with sunflower oil and line with nonstick parchment paper.

Pour the coconut milk into a small saucepan and add the ginger, cardamom pods, star anise, and cinnamon stick. Set over low heat for about 4–5 minutes to gently warm and infuse the milk with the spices—do not allow it to boil. Add the brown sugar, corn syrup, butter, vanilla, and salt. Once the butter has melted and the sugar dissolved, remove from the heat and keep warm.

Pour the superfine sugar into a large (2½-quart) saucepan and add 2 tablespoons water. Warm over low heat to slowly dissolve the sugar without stirring. If any sugar crystals form on the sides of the pan, simply brush them back into the syrup using a clean pastry brush dipped in hot water. Bring the syrup to a boil and continue to cook steadily until it becomes a pale-colored caramel (you may need to gently swirl the pan to ensure that the syrup caramelizes evenly). Working quickly now, reheat the coconut milk mixture until it just comes to a boil. Continue to cook the caramel to a maple-syrup color—this should only take another 30 seconds to 1 minute. Remove the pan from the heat and slowly, steadily, and carefully strain the coconut milk mixture onto the caramel. The mixture will hiss and splutter quite alarmingly, so caution is key here.

Return the pan to the heat and stir until smooth and to dissolve any hardened caramel. Pop the sugar thermometer into the pan and bring the caramel back to a steady boil. Using a heatproof spatula, stir frequently and continue to cook over gentle medium heat until the caramel reaches 244–248°F on the thermometer; this will take about 20–30 minutes, so don't despair if it seems to be taking longer than usual. Remove the pan from the heat, quickly whisk the caramel until smooth, and pour into the prepared pan.

Lightly toast the shredded coconut in a dry frying pan over low heat. Sprinkle over the top of the caramel and leave for at least 4 hours, but preferably overnight, until cold and firm.

Lift the caramel out of the pan and, using a greased or hot kitchen knife, cut into 2-inch x ½-inch fingers. At this stage you could consider dipping the underside of each caramel into melted chocolate and leaving on parchment paper to set. Either way, wrap each caramel in nonstick parchment paper.

Caramel grows up and gets a double dose of chocolate here. Under a crisp, dark chocolate shell lurks a little square of rich, slightly salted caramel with just enough chocolate to count, but not enough to overwhelm. I challenge you to eat just one!

Double Chocolate Caramels

Makes 40–50

sunflower oil, for greasing
¾ cup superfine sugar
⅔ cup brown sugar
3 tablespoons corn syrup
2oz unsalted butter
¾ cup heavy cream plus
　1 tablespoon
3oz dark chocolate
　(64 percent cocoa solids),
　finely chopped
pinch of sea salt flakes
½ teaspoon vanilla bean
　paste

To coat
10oz dark chocolate
　(64 percent cocoa solids),
　finely chopped
tiny chocolate pearls,
　to decorate

Equipment
7-inch square baking pan
sugar thermometer

Store
Caramels will keep for
2 weeks in an airtight
container.

Grease the base and sides of the baking pan with sunflower oil and line with nonstick parchment paper.

Place the superfine sugar, brown sugar, corn syrup, butter, heavy cream, and chocolate in a small saucepan. Add the salt and warm over low to medium heat to dissolve the sugar, melt the butter and chocolate, and heat the cream.

Once the mixture is smooth, pop the sugar thermometer into the pan and bring the mixture to a boil. Continue to cook over steady medium heat until the caramel reaches 244°F on the thermometer. Remove the pan from the heat, add the vanilla, and stir gently once or twice—just enough to combine. Pour the caramel into the prepared pan, spread level with an offset spatula if need be, and leave to cool completely.

Once cold, cover the pan with plastic wrap and leave to set for at least couple of hours or overnight until firm.

Melt the chocolate to coat, or temper according to the instructions on page 24.

Turn the caramel out of the pan onto a sheet of parchment paper. Peel off the lining paper and, using a hot kitchen knife, trim the edges and slice the caramel into neat 1-inch squares.

Using a dipping fork, take one caramel at a time, dip it into the warm melted chocolate, and turn it to coat completely. Lift the caramel out of the chocolate and tap the fork against the side of the bowl to allow any excess chocolate to drip back in. Lay the caramel on a clean sheet of parchment paper, sprinkle the top with chocolate pearls, and repeat with the remaining caramels.

Leave the chocolate-coated caramels in a cool place to set (at least 1 hour) before packaging into boxes.

Nougat,
Nuts, and
Honeycomb

Malted Honeycomb

Hazelnut Caramel Chocolate Bars

Chocolate Peanut Nougat

Cranberry, Cherry, and Pistachio Nougat

Chocolate and Hazelnut Nougat

Almond and Pistachio Turron

Salted Butterscotch Popcorn

Spiced Peanut and Cashew Brittle

Pine Nut and Seed Brittle

Candied Almonds

Nut and Raisin Clusters

*T*his chapter is mostly about nuts. Nuts and sugar. Nuts are one of the most-used ingredients in my candy-making kitchen; they are a perfect pairing for caramel, chocolate, and nougat. I always keep a good variety in my pantry, such as whole and blanched almonds, hazelnuts, pecans, cashews, and peanuts. This means that I can easily whip up a batch of brittle or nougat whenever the urge strikes or need requires.

Almost all of the recipes in this chapter would make ideal gifts. For a stylish and delicious festive gift, cut nougat into bars or squares and package in clear cellophane or waxed bags tied with a ribbon and pretty label. Or try filling small jars with Candied Almonds to make wonderful wedding or party favors.

Salted Butterscotch Popcorn is one of the quickest sweets to make and seems to disappear in less than half the time it takes to make it. I find it is almost impossible to walk past a bowl without sneaking a handful. It might be wise to suggest that you make double the amount that you think you'll need.

There are many different types of nougat, ranging from light, soft, fluffy, and chocolate-coated to firm, sticky, dense with nuts and dried fruit and wrapped in rice paper. In this chapter you'll find all of those and more besides. Nougat is best made the day before you plan on serving it—not only will this make it easier to cut but the flavor will improve after 24 hours.

Brittle and honeycomb are two of the easiest confections to make at home and are perfect to serve at parties. I advise that you be sure to save some for yourself. They're delicious tumbled over ice cream or scattered over a chocolate cake, too… just a thought.

Honeycomb pops up all over the world under a number of different aliases—Hokey Pokey, Cinder Toffee, Yellowman, and Sea Foam—and is quite possibly the one thing guaranteed to strike fear into the heart of every dentist. This is the archenemy—the Voldemort of sugar-based confections. It reminds me of visits to fairgrounds with bright lights, carousels with painted gold horses, and candy stalls with big bags of honeycomb and cotton candy on sticks.

I have added a small amount of malted milk powder to this recipe and coated each piece in milk chocolate, but if you prefer to leave it plain, that works well, too.

Malted *Honeycomb*

Makes about 30 pieces

sunflower oil, for greasing
2 teaspoons baking soda
1¾ cups superfine sugar
4 tablespoons corn syrup
¼ cup honey
1 teaspoon white wine
    vinegar
pinch of salt
1 tablespoon malted milk
    powder
7oz milk chocolate,
    chopped

Grease the baking pan with a little sunflower oil and line the base and sides with nonstick parchment paper. Half-fill the sink with cold water. Sift the baking soda into a small bowl and have a whisk and rubber spatula on stand-by.

Combine the superfine sugar, corn syrup, honey, vinegar, salt and ⅓ cup water into a 2-quart, heavy-bottomed saucepan. Place over low to medium heat, stirring occasionally. Once all of the sugar has dissolved, pop the sugar thermometer into the pan and bring to a boil. Continue to cook at a steady pace until the mixture reaches 284°F. Add the malted milk powder, whisk to combine, and continue to cook to 300°F. Now, working quickly, remove the pan from the heat and plunge the bottom of the pan into the sink of cold water for 5–7 seconds to stop the caramel from cooking any more. Add the baking soda to the pan and whisk for about 5 seconds until thoroughly combined. The caramel will foam quite alarmingly. Still working quickly, use a rubber spatula to scoop the mixture into the prepared pan in an even layer, but do not spread it out, or you will deflate the honeycomb. Leave for a couple of hours to cool and harden.

Put the chocolate in a heatproof bowl and melt over a pan of barely simmering water. Do not allow the bottom of the bowl to touch the water. Stir until smooth, remove from the heat, and leave the chocolate to cool slightly.

Turn the honeycomb out of the pan, peel off the parchment paper, and break into bite-size chunks. Drop a couple of pieces at a time into the melted chocolate to coat, then lift out of the chocolate using a fork, allowing any excess to drip back into the bowl by tapping the fork against the bowl. Set the chocolate-coated honeycomb on a clean sheet of parchment paper and repeat until all of the pieces are coated. Let the chocolate harden before serving.

Equipment
8 x 12-inch baking pan with a depth of 2 inches
sugar thermometer

I really did work at making this recipe yield a smaller quantity, but try as I might, I just couldn't make nougat successfully in smaller amounts. So I guess you'll just have to live with the fact that this makes more than you could ever eat on your own in one sitting—but that's what friends are for!

This recipe might look long and convoluted, but it's simply a question of preparing in stages and should not be rushed. The results are worth it—this is possibly one of my favorite recipes.

Hazelnut Caramel Chocolate Bars

Makes plenty!

For the nougat
1½ cups blanched
   hazelnuts
sunflower oil, for greasing
2 medium egg whites
1¾ cups superfine sugar
pinch of salt
2 tablespoons liquid glucose
pinch of cream of tartar
¼ cup mild-flavored honey
1 teaspoon vanilla extract
   or ½ teaspoon
   vanilla bean paste
14oz milk chocolate,
   chopped

For the caramel
½ cup brown sugar
4 tablespoons corn syrup
3oz unsalted butter
⅔ cup heavy cream
½ cup superfine sugar
1 teaspoon vanilla extract
   or ½ teaspoon vanilla
   bean paste
pinch of sea salt flakes

Equipment
8 x 12-inch baking pan with
   a depth of 2 inches
sugar thermometer

Preheat the oven to 325°F. Spread the hazelnuts on a baking sheet and lightly toast in the oven for 3–4 minutes. Remove from the oven, very roughly chop the nuts (just show the knife to them) and leave to cool.

Grease and line the baking pan with a sheet of nonstick parchment paper. Place the egg whites in the bowl of a freestanding mixer fitted with a whisk attachment, add 1 tablespoon of the superfine sugar and the pinch of salt and set aside for now.

Combine the remaining superfine sugar, liquid glucose, cream of tartar, and ⅓ cup water in a small pan and stir gently over medium heat to dissolve the sugar. Place the sugar thermometer in the pan, bring the syrup to a boil, and continue to cook until it reaches 300°F. Keep a close eye on the temperature, because once it goes over 248°F it will rise very quickly. Place the honey in a small saucepan or heatproof pitcher and warm either over low heat or in the microwave until boiling. Slowly pour the hot honey into the sugar syrup so that the temperature does not drop too quickly, stir well, and continue to cook until the syrup returns to 300°F. Remove the pan from the heat and, working quickly, whisk the egg whites on high speed until medium to stiff peaks form. Reduce the speed of the mixer and slowly pour 2–3 tablespoons of the hot syrup into the egg whites in a slow, steady stream, whisking constantly. If you pour too much syrup too quickly, you could end up shocking the egg whites into scrambling, so pour slowly to begin with. Then steadily add the remainder of the syrup. The mixture will foam up quite dramatically as the hot syrup cooks the whites. Add the vanilla, increase the speed to medium, and continue to whisk for about 2–3 minutes until the mixture is very thick, glossy, and pale. Quickly fold the chopped hazelnuts into the nougat using a rubber spatula.

Scoop the mixture into the prepared pan and spread level using an offset spatula. Don't worry if it's a little uneven and lumpy and bumpy—this will add to its charm later. Cover the nougat with nonstick parchment paper and leave to cool and firm for about 3–4 hours.

Recipe continued overleaf

Store

The bars will keep for up to 1 week in an airtight container.

Melt half the milk chocolate in a heatproof bowl over a pan of barely simmering water, making sure the bottom of the bowl doesn't touch the water. Stir until smooth, then pour over the top of the cold nougat and spread level with an offset spatula. Leave to cool and set firm. Once the chocolate has hardened, lay a large sheet of nonstick parchment paper over the top of the chocolate-covered nougat. Flip the pan over so that the chocolate is now on the bottom. Return the nougat to the pan with the new paper underneath, the chocolate on the underside, and with the paper at least ½-inch higher than the edges of the pan.

To make the caramel, combine the brown sugar, corn syrup, butter, and heavy cream in a small saucepan and place over low–medium heat to melt the butter, dissolve the sugar, and to bring the mixture to a boil. Stir until smooth and remove from the heat. Combine the superfine sugar in a medium-sized pan with 2 tablespoons of water. Set the pan over low heat to dissolve the sugar without stirring. Bring to a boil and cook the syrup until it becomes amber-colored caramel. Remove the pan from the heat and add the hot cream mixture. Stir to combine, pop the sugar thermometer into the pan, and bring the mixture to a steady boil. Continue to cook until the caramel reaches 244°F. Immediately remove the pan from the heat, add the vanilla and salt flakes, stir to combine, and pour the caramel over the nougat in an even layer. Leave to cool.

Once the caramel is completely cold and firm, melt the remaining milk chocolate and pour onto the top of the caramel. Leave until set and hardened before cutting into pieces, squares or bars to serve.

This makes a lighter confection than more traditional nougat recipes, but despite its airiness it's still packed with peanuts, chocolate, and general all-around yumminess. I like to enrobe bite-sized pieces of this nougat in a crisp chocolate coating, but you could half coat them, drizzle them with chocolate, or simply serve them naked (the nougat, that is, not yourself). Pictured on page 141.

Chocolate Peanut Nougat

Makes about 30 pieces

sunflower oil, for greasing
⅔ cup salted roasted
    peanuts
4oz dark chocolate,
    chopped
2 medium egg whites
pinch of salt
½ teaspoon vanilla bean
    paste
1¾ cups superfine sugar
5 tablespoons corn syrup
2 tablespoons liquid glucose
¼ teaspoon cream of tartar
⅓ cup unsweetened
    smooth peanut butter

To coat
9oz dark chocolate,
    chopped
3 tablespoons finely
    chopped salted peanuts

Equipment
8-inch square baking pan
sugar thermometer

Store
The nougat will keep in an airtight container for up to 1 week.

Lightly grease the baking pan with sunflower oil, and line the base and sides with nonstick parchment paper.

Tip the peanuts into a sieve and give them a good shake to remove excess salt; roughly chop, and set aside. Melt the chocolate in a heatproof bowl over a pan of barely simmering water, making sure the bottom of the bowl doesn't touch the water. Stir until smooth and remove from the heat. Place the egg whites, salt, vanilla, and 1 tablespoon of the superfine sugar in the bowl of a freestanding mixer fitted with the whisk attachment, but do not start whisking yet.

Tip the remaining superfine sugar, corn syrup, liquid glucose, and cream of tartar into a 2-quart saucepan. Add ½ cup water and place over low heat. Once the sugar has dissolved, pop the sugar thermometer into the pan and bring to a boil over medium heat. Continue to cook until the syrup reaches 266°F, then start whisking the egg whites on medium–high speed. Continue boiling the syrup and whisking the eggs until the syrup reaches 275°F and the egg whites form stiff peaks—about 20–30 seconds. Remove the hot syrup from the heat and remove the thermometer from the pan. With the mixer on low speed, slowly and steadily add the hot syrup to the egg whites. This should take about 30 seconds and the egg whites will foam up quite dramatically as the hot syrup cooks them. Increase the speed to medium and continue to whisk for about 3–4 minutes until the mixture is stiff, glossy and very white.

Add the peanut butter to the warm melted chocolate, mix until smooth, and fold into the nougat with the chopped peanuts using a rubber spatula until thoroughly combined. Spoon into the prepared pan and spread level with an offset spatula. Cover with parchment paper and using another baking pan, press the surface as flat as you can. Leave the nougat until completely cold.

Melt the chocolate for the coating in a heatproof bowl over a pan of barely simmering water, making sure the bottom of the bowl doesn't touch the water. Stir until smooth, remove from the heat, and leave to cool for a minute.

Turn the nougat out onto a cutting board, peel off the parchment and, using a hot or lightly greased kitchen knife, cut into bite-sized rectangles or squares. Dip each piece, one at a time, into the melted chocolate to coat, then lift out on a dipping or dinner fork, allowing any excess to drip back into the bowl. Carefully place on clean parchment paper and sprinkle with the peanuts. Repeat until all of the nougat is coated. Leave until the chocolate has set and hardened before serving.

This nougat has hints of Christmas about it with its jewel-like red cranberries and green pops of pistachio. You can also set this in a 8 x 12-inch rectangular pan if you'd like to cut the nougat into rectangles rather than wedges. Pictured on page 141.

Cranberry, Cherry, and Pistachio Nougat

Serves 10–12

sunflower oil, for greasing
edible wafer (rice) paper
¾ cup shelled, unsalted
   pistachios
½ cup dried cranberries
⅓ cup dried cherries
⅓ cup shredded coconut
3oz white chocolate
2 medium egg whites
1¾ cups superfine sugar
1 teaspoon vanilla bean
   paste or the seeds from
   ½ vanilla pod
pinch of salt
⅓ cup mild-flavored honey
⅓ cup liquid glucose
¼ teaspoon cream of tartar

Equipment
9-inch springform cake pan
sugar thermometer

Store
Nougat will keep for up to
1 week in an airtight
container between layers of
nonstick parchment paper
and in a cool place.

Lightly grease the cake pan and line the base and sides with nonstick parchment paper. Cover the base of the lined pan with a single, neat layer of wafer paper. Roughly chop the pistachios, combine in a bowl with the cranberries, cherries, and coconut, and set aside. Melt the chocolate in a heatproof bowl over a pan of barely simmering water, making sure the bottom of the bowl doesn't touch the water. Stir until smooth and remove from the heat.

Place the egg whites in the bowl of a freestanding mixer fitted with a whisk attachment, add one tablespoon of the superfine sugar, the vanilla bean paste or seeds, and salt, but do not start whisking yet.

Combine the remaining superfine sugar, honey, liquid glucose, and cream of tartar in a medium saucepan. Add ⅓ cup water and place over medium heat to dissolve the sugar, stirring from time to time. Pop the thermometer into the pan, bring to a boil, and continue to cook until the syrup reaches 284°F. Now start to whisk the egg whites on medium speed until stiff peaks form. Meanwhile, continue to cook the syrup until it reaches 300°F then, working quickly, remove the pan from the heat, remove the thermometer, and with the mixer running on low speed, gradually pour the hot syrup into the beaten egg whites in a slow and steady stream. The egg whites will rise up dramatically as they are cooked in the hot syrup. Increase the mixer speed and continue to whisk for about 3 more minutes until the mixture is thick, stiff, glossy, and pale.

Add the melted chocolate and fruit-and-nut mixture and combine using a rubber spatula. Spoon into the prepared pan and spread level with an offset spatula. Cover with another layer of wafer paper and press the surface level using another slightly smaller cake pan.

Leave until completely cold and firm—a few hours or preferably overnight—before cutting into wedges to serve.

Sometimes I like nougat to be slightly soft and chewy, and that's exactly how it is in this particular recipe. The honey in this nougat just peeks through and rounds the chocolate flavor off, so I would recommend using a mild-flavored honey that won't overpower the chocolate. Edible wafer paper (also called rice paper) comes in a variety of sizes and is available in the baking aisle of larger supermarkets or in some kitchenware stores. Pictured on page 140.

Chocolate and Hazelnut *Nougat*

Makes 30–40 squares

sunflower oil, for greasing
2–4 sheets edible wafer (rice) paper, depending on size
1⅓ cups blanched hazelnuts
6oz dark chocolate (64 percent cocoa solids), chopped
1oz unsalted butter
1 tablespoon cocoa, sifted
1 large egg white
1 teaspoon vanilla bean paste or the seeds of ½ vanilla pod
pinch of salt
1⅔ cups superfine sugar
¾ cup liquid glucose
⅓ cup mild-flavored honey
¼ teaspoon cream of tartar

Equipment
8-inch square baking pan
sugar thermometer

Store
Nougat may be stored in a cool place in an airtight container for up to 1 week.

Preheat the oven to 350°F. Grease the baking pan with sunflower oil and line with nonstick parchment paper.

Cover the base of the lined baking pan with a single layer of wafer paper. Toast the hazelnuts on a baking sheet in the oven for about 4 minutes until lightly golden. Remove the nuts from the oven and very roughly chop them.

Melt the chocolate in a heatproof bowl set over a pan of barely simmering water, making sure the bottom of the bowl doesn't touch the water. Add the butter and cocoa, stir until smooth, and keep warm.

Place the egg white, vanilla bean paste or seeds, and the salt in the bowl of a freestanding mixer fitted with a whisk attachment. Add 1 tablespoon of the superfine sugar, but do not start whisking yet.

Combine the remaining superfine sugar, liquid glucose, honey, and cream of tartar in a medium-sized, heavy-bottomed saucepan and add 4 tablespoons water. Place over medium heat and stir frequently until the sugar has completely dissolved. Pop the sugar thermometer into the pan, bring the syrup to a boil, and cook steadily until it reaches 284°F. Working quickly, remove the pan from the heat and start to whisk the egg white on high speed until stiff peaks form. Turn the whisk to slow-medium speed and pour the hot syrup into the egg whites in a slow and steady stream, being careful that it doesn't splash up the sides of the bowl. Once all of the syrup has been added, continue to whisk for 2–3 minutes until the mixture thickens and turns white and glossy. You may need to scrape the sides of the bowl down with a rubber spatula to ensure that the mixture is evenly combined.

Add the warm chocolate mixture to the bowl and whisk for another 10 seconds until combined. Using a rubber spatula, fold the toasted hazelnuts into the nougat. Scoop into the prepared pan, spread level with an offset spatula and cover the top of the nougat with a single layer of wafer paper, pressing it into an even and smooth surface. Leave to cool completely—about 4 hours or preferably overnight.

Remove the nougat from the pan, peel off the parchment paper, and cut into bars or squares to serve.

Torrone, Turrone, Turron—I say potato, you say patato …

Many countries lay claim to this nougat, but wherever its true origin lies, it ain't the real deal unless it's loaded with honey and almonds.

You need to work quickly and efficiently in this recipe—nougat waits for no man—so have everything measured out and the pan prepared before you even consider starting to boil syrup.

Almond and Pistachio *Turron*

Makes 30–40 pieces

sunflower oil, for greasing
2–4 sheets edible wafer
(rice) paper
1 cup whole almonds
(i.e. skin on)
¾ cup shelled, unsalted
pistachios
2 large egg whites
1½ cups superfine sugar
½ teaspoon vanilla bean
paste or the seeds from
½ vanilla pod
pinch of salt
¾ cup honey
2 tablespoons liquid glucose
¼ teaspoon cream of tartar

Equipment
8-inch square baking pan
sugar thermometer

Store
The turron will keep in an
airtight container for
1 week.

Grease the baking pan with sunflower oil and line with nonstick parchment paper. Preheat the oven to 325°F.

Cover the base of the lined baking pan with a single layer of edible wafer paper— you may need to trim the wafer paper to fit the pan exactly.

Lightly toast the nuts on a baking sheet in the oven for 3–4 minutes. Allow to cool slightly, then chop.

Place the egg whites, 1 tablespoon superfine sugar, the vanilla paste or seeds, and salt into the bowl of a freestanding mixer fitted with a whisk attachment and leave to one side for now.

Warm the honey in a small saucepan over low heat until just boiling. Remove from the heat and keep warm. Combine the remaining superfine sugar, liquid glucose, cream of tartar, and ⅓ cup water in another pan and stir gently over low heat to dissolve the sugar. Pop the sugar thermometer into the pan, bring the syrup to a boil, and continue to cook until it reaches 300°F. Remove the pan from the heat, carefully add the hot honey, stir well, return to the heat and continue to cook until the syrup returns to 300°F. Remove the pan from the heat and, working quickly, whisk the egg whites on high speed until stiff peaks form. Reduce the speed of the mixer slightly, and gently pour the hot honey syrup into the egg whites in a slow, steady stream, whisking constantly. The mixture will foam up dramatically as the hot syrup cooks the egg whites. Increase the speed to medium and continue to whisk for about another 3 minutes until the mixture is very thick and a pale buttermilk color. Fold the chopped nuts in using a rubber spatula.

Quickly scoop the mixture into the prepared pan and spread into a smooth, even layer using an offset spatula. Press a single layer of wafer paper on top of the Turron, flatten the surface completely using another baking pan, and weigh the top down with a couple of cans. Leave to cool overnight.

The next day, when the turron is completely cold, turn it out of the pan and onto a cutting board. Peel off the parchment paper and, using a greased kitchen knife, cut into strips or squares to serve. You can also cut it into bars and wrap in cellophane for a delicious festive gift.

No matter how much popcorn you make, it will always disappear in a flash, and this butterscotch variety is no exception. The butterscotch hardens around the popcorn as it cools, enveloping each piece in a crisp shell with just a hint of vanilla and sea salt. Try adding roughly chopped salted peanuts, dark chocolate chips, or even mini marshmallows to the mix for even more indulgence. Movie nights just got a whole lot more tasty.

My only advice is that once it has cooled, put the popcorn in a jar, put the lid on really tight, and put the jar on a shelf really high up, or you will find that fingers will wander into the bowl for just one more morsel and the whole batch will have disappeared without your noticing.

Salted Butterscotch *Popcorn*

Serves 2–6

2 tablespoons sunflower oil
½ cup popcorn kernels
¾ cup superfine sugar
3oz unsalted butter
1 teaspoon vanilla extract
generous pinch of sea-salt
 flakes

Store

Popcorn can be stored in an airtight container for up to 1 week, though I doubt that this is something you'll need to know.

Place the sunflower oil in a large, deep saucepan over medium–high heat. Add the popcorn kernels to the pan, cover with a tight-fitting lid, and wait for the popping to start, shaking the pan from time to time. Continue to cook the popcorn and shake the pan until the popping stops, then immediately remove from the heat and transfer the popped corn into a large bowl, picking out any unpopped kernels as you do so.

Place the superfine sugar in a medium-sized, heavy-bottomed saucepan and add 1–2 tablespoons water. Set over medium heat to dissolve the sugar without stirring. You may need to swirl the syrup gently and brush down the sides of the pan with cold water to ensure that the sugar dissolves evenly without crystallizing either on the bottom or sides of the pan. Once the sugar has dissolved, bring the syrup to a boil and continue to cook steadily until it starts to caramelize and turn a beautiful, deep golden amber color. Remove the pan from the heat and add the butter, vanilla extract, and salt, being careful as the caramel will splutter as you do so. Swirl the pan to melt the butter into the caramel and return to low heat for another 20 seconds to combine the mixture evenly.

Quickly pour the butterscotch over the popcorn and mix together using two forks, so that the popcorn is evenly coated and starts to stick together in small clusters. Transfer the butterscotch popcorn to a large baking sheet to cool before serving.

Spiced Peanut and Cashew *Brittle*

Makes about 30 pieces

1 cup unsalted peanuts
1 cup unsalted cashews
½ cup brown sugar
1¼ cups superfine sugar
5 tablespoons corn syrup
2oz unsalted butter
½ rounded teaspoon
  baking soda
½ teaspoon vanilla bean
  paste
½ rounded teaspoon
  smoked paprika
½ teaspoon ground
  cinnamon
large pinch of sea salt flakes

Preheat the oven to 350°F.

Lightly toast the nuts on a large baking sheet in the oven for 3–4 minutes until pale golden. Tip the nuts into a bowl and leave to cool. Cover the baking sheet with a sheet of nonstick parchment paper.

Combine both sugars in a medium saucepan. Add the corn syrup and ½ cup water and warm over medium heat to dissolve the sugar. Add the butter, stir until melted, and bring to a boil. Pop the sugar thermometer into the pan and cook steadily until the temperature reaches 310°F. Remove the pan from the heat, and add the baking soda, vanilla, smoked paprika, cinnamon, and salt. Add the nuts and stir well to combine (the mixture will foam up as you mix). Spoon onto the prepared baking sheet and spread level with the back of the spoon.

Leave the brittle until completely cold and hardened (at least 1 hour) before breaking into pieces to serve.

Pine Nut and Seed *Brittle*

Makes 20–30 pieces

¾ cup pine nuts
⅓ cup mixed seeds
  (pumpkin and sunflower)
1¼ cups superfine sugar
1oz unsalted butter
2 tablespoons honey or
  corn syrup
pinch of sea salt flakes
1 teaspoon orange-flower
  water (optional)

Equipment
Both recipes require a
sugar thermometer

Store
Spiced Peanut and Cashew
Brittle will keep in an airtight
container between layers
of nonstick paper for up
to 2 weeks.
Pine Nut and Seed Brittle
will keep in the same
conditions for up to 1 week.

Preheat the oven to 325°F.

Tip the pine nuts on to a large baking sheet and lightly toast in the oven for 3–4 minutes until just golden. Transfer in a bowl and add the mixed seeds. Line the baking sheet with nonstick parchment.

In a heavy-bottomed pan, combine the sugar with ⅓ cup water and place over medium heat to dissolve the sugar. Add the butter and honey (or syrup) and stir until melted. Pop the sugar thermometer into the pan and bring to a boil. Continue to cook over medium heat until the mixture reaches 349°F (It can feel like an eternity for the mixture to reach the right temperature, but once it goes over 284°F it will shoot up quickly, so be prepared to move swiftly when the moment arises.)

Remove the pan from the heat, add the salt and orange-flower water (if using), and stir to combine. Add the nuts and seeds and quickly mix, so that they are evenly coated in the caramel. Scoop onto the lined baking sheet and spread level with the back of a spoon or offset spatula. Leave until completely cold and hardened before breaking into pieces to serve.

Toasted whole almonds are coated here in a crisp caramel shell before being enrobed in chocolate. To finish I like to dust them in a freeze-dried cherry powder and sugar mix, which really does bring something rather special to the party. If you like things simpler though, go for the confectioner's sugar or cocoa dusting option; the result will still be delicious—just a shade less jazzy. Freeze-dried fruit is available online or in some specialist grocery stores and comes in a variety of flavors, but cherry is quite possibly my favorite, and I'm always looking for different ways to use it.

Candied Almonds

Makes enough to fill 3–4 jars

1½ cups whole almonds
½ cup superfine sugar
⅔ tablespoon unsalted butter
5oz dark chocolate, chopped
9oz milk chocolate, chopped

To coat
2 tablespoons freeze-dried cherry powder
2–3 tablespoons confectioner's sugar
2 tablespoons cocoa

Equipment
pair of thick Latex food-grade gloves

Store
Candied almonds will keep in an airtight container for up to 1 month.

Preheat the oven to 325°F and line the baking sheet with parchment paper.

Tip the almonds onto another baking sheet and toast in the oven for 3–4 minutes. Meanwhile, put the superfine sugar in a small heavy-bottomed saucepan, add 1 tablespoon of water and warm over low to medium heat to dissolve the sugar without stirring. Use a clean pastry brush dipped in hot water to brush away and dissolve any crystals that form on the sides of the pan. Bring the syrup to a boil and continue to cook steadily until it becomes a honey-colored caramel. Because of the small amount of caramel that you are making, this will take no time at all. Pour the warm almonds into the pan, remove from the heat, and stir to coat each one in the liquid caramel. Add the butter and stir to combine.

Working quickly, pour the nuts onto the prepared baking sheet. Put on the Latex gloves and toss the almonds around in your hands, using your fingers to separate them out so that each one is enrobed in a smooth, crisp caramel jacket. Leave to cool and harden at room temperature.

Once the almonds are completely cold, transfer them to a medium-sized bowl and chill in the fridge for 15 minutes while you melt the chocolate. Combine the dark and milk chocolate in a heatproof bowl and melt over a pan of barely simmering water, making sure the bottom of the bowl doesn't touch the water. Stir until smooth, remove from the heat, and cool slightly.

Combine the freeze-dried cherry powder with 1 teaspoon of the confectioner's sugar and spread on a large plate. Put the remaining confectioner's sugar on another plate and the cocoa on to a third.

Spoon one-third of the melted chocolate onto the cooled almonds and, working quickly, stir well to coat each nut in chocolate. Transfer the almonds back to the covered baking sheet and separate them out again. Chill again for 5 minutes. Repeat this coating and chilling twice more until all the chocolate has been used.

Before the final chocolate coating hardens, toss the almonds in either the cherry powder, confectioner's sugar, or cocoa.

These fruity, nutty little numbers couldn't be much easier to put together. Feel free to swap the fruit and nuts around as you see fit, or according to what you have on hand. Pistachios, pecans, dried cranberries, apricots, and golden raisins would all be perfect substitutions.

Nut and Raisin *Clusters*

Makes about 12 large clusters

¾ cup blanched almonds
¾ cup blanched hazelnuts
½ cup raisins
½ cup dried sour cherries
¼ cup superfine sugar
1 tablespoon dark rum
7oz dark chocolate, chopped

Store
Nut and Raisin Clusters will keep for 1–2 weeks in an airtight container between layers of parchment paper.

Preheat the oven to 350°F.

Roughly chop the almonds and hazelnuts and spread on a baking sheet. Lightly toast the nuts in the oven for about 4 minutes. Meanwhile, roughly chop the raisins and dried cherries.

Combine the superfine sugar in a small pan with 1 tablespoon water. Set the pan over medium heat to dissolve the sugar. Bring to a boil, simmer for 1 minute until syrupy, add the rum, and bring back to a boil.

Add the dried fruit to the toasted nuts and mix well. Quickly pour on the hot syrup and mix to coat the fruit and nuts. Allow the mixture to cool for a moment and then, using your hands, shape the fruit and nuts into 12 evenly sized mounds. Arrange on nonstick parchment paper and leave to cool.

Melt the chocolate in a heatproof bowl over a pan of barely simmering water, making sure the bottom of the bowl doesn't touch the water. Remove from the heat and stir until smooth. Place one nut cluster at a time on the tines of a fork and dip into the melted chocolate to cover. Lift out of the chocolate, tapping the fork on the side to allow any excess chocolate to drip back into the bowl. Place on parchment paper and repeat until all of the clusters are coated in chocolate.

Leave in a cool place until the chocolate has set and hardened before serving.

Hard Candy

Lemon and Orange Drops

Raspberry Drops

Candy Buttons

Crystal Candy Sticks

Candy with Lollipop Dippers

Violet Candies

Aniseed Twists

Candy Canes

This chapter is a collection of recipes that I imagine are most likely to appeal to children, or at least to the big kid in all of us. I think that there is something rather nostalgic and old-fashioned about hard candy—maybe it's the rows of shiny glass jars in the candy shop, each filled with different shapes, flavors, and colors that were so captivating to me as a small child.

Hard candy should be brightly colored and sharply flavored using extracts and oils. I prefer to use natural flavorings when possible, such as orange, lemon, rose, violet, and peppermint, and fresh fruit juices. With a few small jars of food-coloring paste, you can create candy in a rainbow of shades to match just about any flavor imaginable. Just remember that a tiny amount goes a long way.

Crystal Candy Sticks are almost guaranteed to get most kids (big and small alike) excited—most candy making is part cooking and part science but this recipe is almost all about science. Making sugar crystals from brightly colored sugar syrup is an exercise in patience, too—they can take a couple of weeks to form but the wait is more than worth it.

A quicker way to get your candy fix would be to make bright-colored, glassy lollipops. Lollipop sticks and molds are widely available in good kitchenware stores or online in many shapes and sizes.

I saw something similar to these little citrusy drops in a shop in Paris and was determined to set about making my own.

Many supermarkets now stock good-quality lemon and orange extract—cheap imitation flavoring really will not do. There is also a small amount of citric acid in this recipe that gives the candies an extra sharpness—it is often used in recipes for homemade cordials and you'll find it in pharmacies or specialist grocery stores.

You will need a sugar thermometer and some quiet kitchen time, but no other fancy equipment for making these tangy little drops, although you might find another pair of hands helpful to assist in pulling and cutting the candy mixture.

Lemon and Orange *Drops*

Makes about 70 small drops

sunflower oil, for greasing
1 cup plus 1 tablespoon
    superfine sugar
½ teaspoon cream of tartar
1 teaspoon citric acid
1 teaspoon lemon or orange
    extract
yellow or orange food-
    coloring paste
1 tablespoon confectioner's
    sugar

Equipment
sugar thermometer

Store
Lemon and Orange Drops
will keep for 1–2 weeks
in glass jars in a cool,
dry place.

Prepare your equipment and measure all of the ingredients before you start, because once the sugar is boiling you will need to work quickly. Line a large baking sheet with a large sheet of nonstick parchment paper and grease well with sunflower oil. Grease an offset spatula and some kitchen scissors with oil, too.

Combine the sugar, cream of tartar, and ⅓ cup water in a small to medium-sized, heavy-bottomed saucepan and bring slowly to a boil, stirring frequently to completely dissolve the sugar. Pop the sugar thermometer into the pan and continue to boil over medium heat for about 5 minutes until the syrup reaches 300°F. Do not be tempted to walk away from the pan or do anything else while the sugar is coming up to temperature—it can easily and quickly go over and above the required temperature. As soon as the syrup comes to temperature, remove the pan from the heat. Working quickly, add the citric acid, lemon (or orange) extract, and food-coloring paste and swirl or stir to combine thoroughly. You will only need a tiny amount of food coloring as a little goes a long way.

Pour the syrup out onto the greased parchment paper and leave to cool for 1–2 minutes or until a light skin has formed on the top. Use the greased offset spatula to lift the edges of the syrup off the paper and flip it into the middle, working the syrup up and over and back on itself until it cools, thickens, and becomes tacky. Once it is cool enough to handle, quickly gather the candy in your hands and pull it into a thick rope. Join the ends together and twist it into a thick rope. Pull the ends apart and repeat this pulling and twisting until the rope starts to lighten in color, firm, and cool. Stretch the candy into a rope just between ½ and 1 inch in diameter. Using the greased scissors, snip the candy into little triangular nuggets onto a baking sheet. (If at any point the candy becomes too hard and brittle to cut, place it on a parchment-covered baking sheet and warm in a low oven for 10–20 seconds until pliable.)

Toss the drops in confectioner's sugar to prevent them from sticking together and, once completely cold, store in jars.

These little drops are flavored with real raspberry juice and I love to make them in assorted shapes and sizes. Although not strictly necessary, I like to add a tiny dot of red food-coloring paste to the mixture—just enough to give these candies a clearer, brighter finish.

Raspberry Drops

Makes about 40, depending on the size of the molds

cake release spray or
   sunflower oil, for greasing
2½ cups raspberries
juice of ½ lemon
1½ cups superfine sugar,
   plus 2 tablespoons
⅓ cup liquid glucose
¼ teaspoon cream of tartar
red food-coloring paste
   (optional)

Equipment
assorted candy molds
sugar thermometer

Store
Raspberry Drops will keep in a cool, dry place in an airtight jar for 3–4 days.

Grease the candy molds, using either cake release spray or sunflower oil.

Combine the raspberries in a small pan with the lemon juice and the 2 tablespoons superfine sugar. Warm over low heat to dissolve the sugar and continue to cook very gently until the raspberries break down, releasing a lot of juice. Remove from the heat and leave for 30 minutes to cool and for the berries to release more juice. Pour into a fine mesh sieve over a bowl and leave for about 2 hours to drain without pushing, pressing, or mixing the fruit (otherwise you will have a raspberry puree, rather than a clear ruby-red juice). You should end up with around ½ cup of raspberry juice.

Combine the remaining superfine sugar, the liquid glucose, cream of tartar, and ½ cup water in a medium-sized, heavy-bottomed saucepan. Bring slowly to a boil, stirring gently to dissolve the sugar. Pop the sugar thermometer into the pan and continue to cook until the syrup reaches 310°F.

Meanwhile, pour the raspberry juice into another small pan, bring to a boil, and simmer until reduced by half. As soon as the syrup comes up to temperature, remove the pan from the heat. Very carefully and slowly, pour the hot raspberry juice into the syrup—it will bubble furiously. Stir gently to combine and return the pan to the heat, bringing the contents back to a boil and cooking steadily until the mixture returns to 310°F. Working quickly, add a drop of food-coloring paste, if using, and mix to combine evenly. Pour the hot syrup into a warmed heatproof pitcher and carefully pour into the greased molds. Leave until set solid. The drops should slip out of the molds easily once they are set.

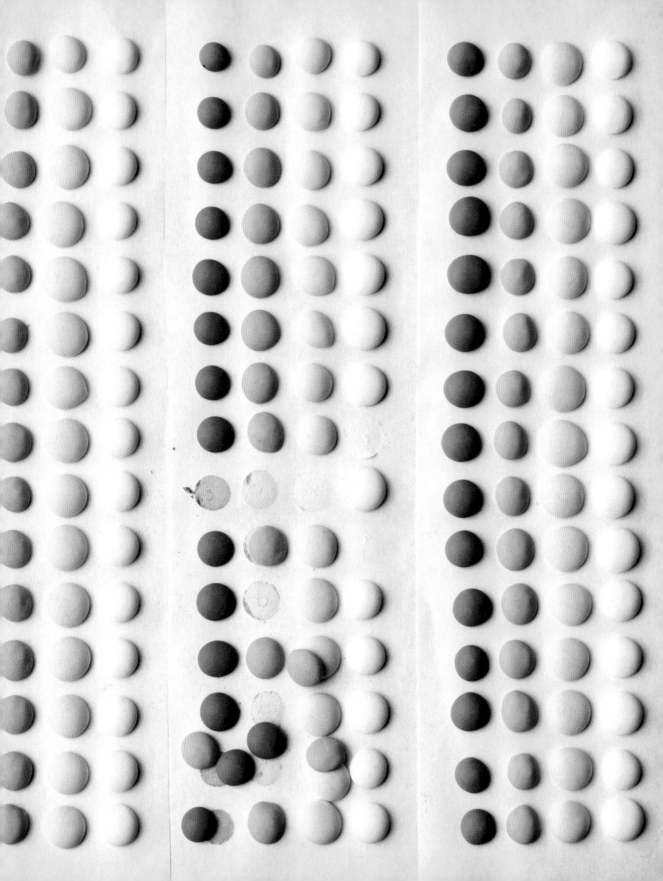

The variations on these little dots of sweetness are endless—they can be made in all the colors of the rainbow and in as many flavors as you can imagine. I prefer to use natural flavors for my candy making, but you can use whatever tickles your fancy—bubblegum, lemonade, cherry…

Try color coordinating your Candy Buttons to a party theme and packaging each sheet of dots in pretty cellophane bags with labels and ribbons. Birthdays, Christmas, Halloween, Valentine's Day—there isn't an occasion that wouldn't benefit from these little gems.

Candy *Buttons*

Makes about 720 small buttons

1 tablespoon powdered
  egg whites
2–2¼ cups confectioner's
  sugar
natural flavoring such
  as lemon, orange, rose,
  or violet
4 different food-coloring
  pastes

Equipment
plain paper and a
  marker
freezer paper sheets
disposable piping bags

Store
Candy Buttons will keep for up to 2 weeks in an airtight box or jar.

If you are going for neat strips of candy buttons, you will need to start by making paper templates. Take a sheet of white paper and a magic marker. On the paper make 2 grids of dots with the marker. Each grid should be 4 rows across and 15 down in neat lines, with each dot about ½ inch from the next. Photocopy this sheet 6 times.

Lay the templates out on a large table or work surface. Tape a sheet of freezer paper, shiny side down, onto each template sheet so that it is completely covered and so that you can see the dots though the paper. You are now ready to start.

Mix the egg-white powder with ¼ cup cold water and most of the confectioner's sugar and beat until thick and smooth. The mixture should drop off the spoon into a smooth mound that holds its shape without peaking—add more water or sugar by the teaspoonful in order to get the correct consistency.

Add your chosen flavoring—you will only need a few drops—and mix well. Divide the mixture among 4 bowls and add a tiny dot of different food coloring to each bowl, mixing well until combined. Spoon the mixtures into separate piping bags and twist the tops to prevent any mixture spilling out. Using one color at a time, snip the end of the piping bag into a fine nozzle and pipe a row of dots on each grid, using the template as a guide. Repeat with the remaining colors.

Leave the Candy Buttons to dry overnight in a cool, dry place and then cut into strips and package the strips in clear party bags to serve.

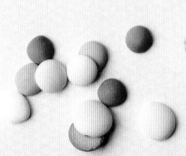

For this recipe, sugar-crusted bamboo skewers are suspended in a jar of saturated sugar solution and the sugar crystals then form around the stick to create a rather beautiful, sculptural treat. Don't be tempted to disturb the candy sticks until they have formed large crystals, as pictured— this can take up to two weeks (or maybe even longer in cooler climates). These are not for the impatient among us, but the results are so satisfyingly beautiful that they make the wait more than worth it. If you are planning to make these crystals for a specific occasion, I would suggest starting well in advance, since they will keep for months.

Crystal Candy Sticks

Makes 4–6

3½ cups superfine sugar
food-coloring paste

Equipment
10 clean wooden skewers
2 wide-necked jars

Store
Candy Sticks will keep for months in an airtight box in a cool, dry place.

Take 6 of the skewers and dip into a glass of cold water so that the water comes around 4 inches up the skewers.

Put ½ cup of the sugar on a baking sheet and roll the wet end of each skewer in the sugar to coat evenly. Stand, sugared end uppermost, (taking care not to knock any sugar off) in an empty glass for about 2 hours to dry.

Combine the remaining sugar with 1 cup water in a saucepan and, over low to medium heat, gently stir to completely dissolve the sugar. Bring to a boil and simmer gently for 2–3 minutes until very slightly thickened and syrupy.

Add enough food-coloring paste to the syrup to make a good, strong color, stir well, and divide between the jars. Leave the syrup to cool for about 1 hour.

Lay 2 clean wooden skewers across the top of each jar in a parallel line roughly an inch apart. Clamp a clothespin or food-bag clip onto each of the sugar-coated skewers roughly halfway up, being careful not to knock off any of the dried sugar. Sink the sugared ends of the skewers into the syrup and adjust the height of the clothespin so that the sugar skewer hovers, suspended, roughly ½ inch from the bottom of the jar. Then rest the clothespin astride the parallel skewers. Repeat with the remaining sugar skewers, so that you have 3 per jar and each skewer is spaced well apart. Leave the jars undisturbed in a warm, dry place (a sunny windowsill is perfect) for at least 1 week, until large sugar crystals have formed around the submerged skewers. The timings of the crystal formation will vary depending on the room temperature and light and can take up to 3 weeks in cooler climates.

Carefully remove the skewers from the jars, allowing the excess syrup to drip back into the jar. A layer of sugar-crystal crust may have formed on the top of the jars so be careful not to knock any crystals off your skewers as you extract them from the jar. Leave the skewers, suspended crystal-end down over a glass, to dry for at least 1 hour.

This recipe is pure nostalgia. I have vivid memories of eating powdered candy from little packages with a lollipop dipper. Somehow one always used to run out before you could finish the other—usually the stick went first and then you tipped the powder right from the package into your mouth for a full-on sugar fizz sensation.

Look for lollipop molds in different shapes and sizes and remember to grease them well. You could also make free-form lollipops by spooning the syrup onto greased parchment paper.

Candy with Lollipop Dippers

Makes 12

For the powder
2½ cups superfine sugar
2 teaspoons citric acid
1 teaspoon baking soda
a few drops of lemon or orange extract
yellow and pink food-coloring pastes
natural raspberry flavoring

For the lollipop dippers
sunflower oil, for greasing
1½ cups granulated sugar
8 tablespoons corn syrup
½ teaspoon cream of tartar
1 teaspoon orange or lemon extract
red or pink food-coloring paste

Equipment
12-hole small lollipop mold (optional)
sugar thermometer
lollipop sticks

Make the powder first. Tip the superfine sugar into the bowl of a food processor and blend for 1 minute until the sugar is finely ground. Add the citric acid and baking soda and blend again to combine thoroughly. Pour half of the powder into a bowl and set aside. Add a few drops of lemon (or orange) extract to the food processor bowl and a tiny amount of yellow food-coloring paste. Blend again until thoroughly combined and the powder turns a delicate pastel color. Remove from the food processor and repeat with the reserved powder, this time adding pink food coloring and raspberry flavoring. Store in airtight jars until ready to serve.

Grease the lollipop molds with sunflower oil or line a baking sheet with greased parchment paper.

Combine the sugar and corn syrup in a small, heavy-bottomed saucepan. Add the cream of tartar and ¾ cup water and warm over medium heat to dissolve the sugar, stirring frequently. Pop the sugar thermometer into the pan and bring the syrup to a boil. Continue to cook steadily over medium heat until the syrup reaches 310°F on the sugar thermometer. Immediately remove the pan from the heat, add the extract and a tiny amount of food-coloring paste to the syrup, and stir until evenly mixed.

Pour the mixture into the prepared molds and place a stick in each lollipop. If you don't have lollipop molds, simply leave the syrup to cool and thicken slightly, then spoon onto greased parchment paper in neat circles and place a lollipop stick into the middle of each circle. Leave to set until solid and completely cold before removing from the molds or parchment.

To serve, pour the powder into little jars or pretty waxed bags and serve with the lollipop dippers.

Store
The powder will keep for up to 1 month in an airtight jar in a cool, dry place. Lollipops are best served 1–2 days after making and can be stored in individual cellophane bags at cool room temperature.

I was gazing into my garden and admiring my beautiful pots of violas and violets when I remembered seeing flower lollipops on Sprinkle Bakes blog and was inspired to try something similar.

This is my version of violet drops that are made in either candy molds or in DIY molds that require nothing more than a tray of confectioner's sugar and cornstarch.

If you prefer, you could flavor these drops with rose oil, rosewater or rose extract, color the mixture a subtle shade of pink, and drop a small fresh or dried rose petal into each piece of candy. As always when using fresh flowers in cooking, please make sure that they are nontoxic, haven't been sprayed with chemicals, and are preferably picked from your own garden.

Violet Candies

Makes about 70, depending on the size of the molds

4 cups confectioner's sugar (optional)
1½ cups cornstarch (optional)
sunflower oil, for greasing (optional)
1½ cups superfine sugar
¾ cup liquid glucose
¼ teaspoon citric acid
few drops violet extract or oil
violet/mauve food-coloring paste
edible violets

Equipment
12 x 16-inch baking sheet (optional) or assorted candy molds
sugar thermometer

Store
Violet Candies will keep in a cool, dry place in an airtight jar or tin for up to 1 month.

If you want to make your own molds, simply mix the confectioner's sugar and cornstarch until thoroughly combined. Tip into a 12 x 16-inch baking sheet and pack into a smooth, firm layer. This is easiest to do by placing another baking sheet on top and pressing down firmly. Using a small patterned implement, such as a decorative button or sugar paste embosser, press into the packed sugar mixture to create indents in neat rows.

If you are using ready-made molds, grease them lightly with sunflower oil.

To make the Violet Candies, combine the sugar and liquid glucose in a small, heavy-bottomed saucepan. Add ⅔ cup water and warm the pan over medium heat to dissolve the sugar, stirring frequently. Pop the sugar thermometer into the pan and bring the syrup to a boil. Continue to cook steadily over medium heat until the syrup reaches 310°F. Immediately remove the pan from the heat, add the citric acid, violet extract, and a tiny amount of food-coloring paste to the syrup. Stir until evenly mixed.

Pour the hot syrup into a warmed measuring pitcher and carefully pour into the prepared molds. Leave to cool for a minute or two and, if using fresh flowers, use clean tweezers to carefully push one flower or petal into each candy and leave until completely cold and set solid.

Remove from the molds to serve.

The very best of old-fashioned candies and possibly the closest the home candymaker will come to making aniseed balls with their polished bright red candy shell and anise seed in the center. If you happen to have any willing helpers within earshot, I would holler loudly and enlist their services. Two pairs of hands are better than one when it comes to cutting and twisting.

Anise seeds and extract/oil are available in specialist grocers or online.

Aniseed *Twists*

Makes about 70 pieces

sunflower oil, for greasing
2 tablespoons
   confectioner's sugar
1½ cups superfine sugar
8 tablespoons corn syrup
pinch of cream of tartar
1 teaspoon anise seeds
¼ teaspoon citric acid
a few drops aniseed extract
   or oil
red food-coloring paste

Equipment
2 large baking sheets
sugar thermometer

Store
Aniseed Twists will keep for up to 1 month in an airtight jar or tin in a cool, dry place.

Preheat the oven to 225°F. Grease a sheet of parchment paper with sunflower oil and use it to line one of the baking sheets. Spread the confectioner's sugar on the second baking sheet.

In a medium-sized, heavy-bottomed saucepan, combine the superfine sugar, corn syrup, cream of tartar, anise seeds, and ½ cup water. Warm over low to medium heat, stirring gently to completely dissolve the sugar. Pop a sugar thermometer into the pan, bring the syrup to a boil, and continue to cook steadily until it reaches 300°F.

Remove the pan from the heat and, working quickly, add the citric acid, along with the aniseed extract or oil and a dot of red food-coloring paste. Mix well until thoroughly combined and the syrup is a deep red color. Pour onto the greased parchment paper and leave for about 5–10 minutes (depending on the temperature of your kitchen) until it starts to form a skin and is cool enough to handle.

Using a greased offset spatula, flip the edges of the mixture off the paper and back into the middle of the syrup. Continue to do this until the mixture thickens enough to be lifted in your hands. By now, it should be cool and firm enough to handle easily, so take half of the syrup in your hands and pull it into a rope about 2 inches wide. Join the ends together and twist the rope so that it is now twice as thick. Pull the ends again to stretch them out, fold together and twist again. Repeat this pulling, twisting, and stretching until the candy is cool and firm but still malleable. Now is the time to call for helpers.

Pull or roll the candy rope out to a thickness of just under an inch, and, using clean scissors, snip into 1-inch lengths. Twist the ends of each piece of candy a couple of times and then drop into the confectioner's sugar to coat. Repeat with the remaining half of the candy. If the candy becomes too hard to handle, warm it in a low oven on the greased paper for 30 seconds to 1 minute until pliable again. Leave the Aniseed Twists to harden and cool before packaging into jars or tins.

Who doesn't love Candy Canes? These say Christmas more than any other candy, and no Christmas stocking or gift is complete without one. Once you've become skilled at making candy canes, you could try adding in a third color twist—now that would really impress Santa!

Candy Canes

Makes about 12

sunflower oil, for greasing
1 cup superfine sugar
2 tablespoons liquid glucose
½ teaspoon cream of tartar
1 teaspoon peppermint
    extract
red food-coloring paste

Equipment
sugar thermometer

Store
Candy Canes are best served no more than 1–2 days after making. They should be individually wrapped in cellophane and stored in a cool, dry place.

Preheat the oven to 250°F.

Prepare your equipment and measure all of the ingredients before you begin, because once the sugar is boiling you will need to work quickly. Cover two baking sheets with nonstick parchment paper and grease the paper well with sunflower oil. Grease an offset spatula and some kitchen scissors with oil, too.

Combine the sugar, liquid glucose, cream of tartar, and ⅓ cup water in a small to medium-sized, heavy-bottomed saucepan and bring slowly to a boil, stirring frequently to completely dissolve the sugar. Pop the sugar thermometer into the pan. Continue to boil over medium heat for about 5 minutes until the syrup reaches 300°F. Do not be tempted to walk away from the pan or do anything else while the sugar is coming up to temperature—it can easily and quickly go over and above the required heat. As soon as the syrup comes to temperature, working quickly, remove the pan from the heat, add the peppermint extract, and mix to combine.

Divide the syrup evenly between the prepared baking sheets, add a tiny drop of red food coloring to one sheet, and leave both to cool for about 1 minute or until a light skin has formed on the top. Working on one sheet at a time and starting with the plain syrup, use the greased offset spatula to lift the edges of the syrup up and over and back on itself until it cools, thickens, and becomes tacky. Once it is cool enough to handle, quickly gather the candy in your hands and pull it into a thick rope, twisting it back on itself and pulling it back into a rope again. Repeat this pulling and twisting until the rope starts to lighten in color and becomes white, firm, and cool. Pull the white candy into an inch-thick rope and place on the greased paper. Repeat with the red candy mixture. You want both the red and white candy ropes to be the same thickness and temperature. You can pop the white candy into the warm oven for 30 seconds to warm it again if you need to.

Lay the red candy rope on top of the white and roll them gently on the work surface so that they stick together. Start to twist one end so that the colors merge into a spiral—you may need to gently pull the ends to lengthen and thin the candy as you do this. Using the greased scissors, snip the candy into 6-inch lengths and bend one end of each piece into the distinctive candy cane shape. Place on a clean sheet of nonstick parchment paper and leave until cold and hard.

If at any point the candy becomes too hard and brittle, place it on a parchment paper-covered baking sheet and warm in the oven for 10–20 seconds until pliable again.

Gift Packaging

If you are making candies and chocolates to give as gifts, then you've already gone to some effort. But with a touch more creativity, you can take your sweet delights to a whole new level.

I collect jars, boxes, and tins, often recycled from other uses, that are perfect to fill with homemade candies and give as gifts. Look out for vintage glass candy jars at antique fairs or online. They not only look beautiful on your kitchen shelves but, when filled with homemade candies, make a doubly delightful gift. I rather like filling mini jars with a small scoop of candied almonds or truffles for wedding favors, party gifts, or table presents.

I keep a box filled with ribbon and scraps that can be used to embellish sweetie gift packages—some ribbons are new, some vintage, and some are on their third or even fourth incarnation. I find it impossible to walk by a fabric store without popping in to add a length of ribbon to my growing collection.

Old-fashioned brown paper luggage labels give a vintage feel to boxes and packages. Rubber ink stamps can now be found in hundreds of different graphics, shapes, and patterns, and ink pads come in just about all the colors of the rainbow and are a wonderful way of decorating labels and boxes. If you were to get serious about foodie gift parcels,

you could consider having your own customized ink stamp made.

Clear cellophane bags are available in craft stores in a range of sizes, from ones that will hold one or two truffles up to family-size bags. They are great for candies that are unlikely to stick together, such as chocolate truffles, marshmallows, popcorn, or chocolate-coated honeycomb. Just be sure that all packaging is clean and food-safe before use.

Look out for miniature wooden pins or clips in stationers to secure the tops of party favor bags in a novel fashion. Pretty patterned bags are now available in craft stores or online in a dazzling array of colors and patterns but are very easy to make yourself. All you need is some pretty paper, nonstick parchment paper to line the bags, and nontoxic glue to seal the edges.

Make sure that you include storage and serving instructions with all of your gift packages—some truffles are best stored in the fridge, served at room temperature and eaten within a few days, while other candies are best eaten immediately.

Suppliers

Chocolate
www.chocolatetradingco.com
Tel: +44 1625 508224

A fantastic selection of quality
chocolate including Valrhona.

Mixers and kitchen hardware
www.kitchenaid.com

Electric stand mixers—essential
equipment for ease in making
marshmallows and nougat.

Good quality vanilla pods
www.vanillaqueen.com

Freeze-dried fruit
www.northbaytrading.com

Candy thermometers
www.amazon.com
www. williams-sonoma.com

Candy and chocolate molds
www.kitchencrafts.com
www.michaels.com
www.sweettreatsupply.com
www.confectioneryhouse.com

Birch teaspoons
www.webstaurantstore.com

Kitchen equipment
www.amazon.com
www.surlatable.com

Index

Acknowledgments

I have loved every minute spent creating this book —from the initial thoughts and ideas, through to writing, and endless testing and tasting, fun-filled days of photography, and the final editing. But none of this would have been possible without a number of incredibly talented folk. So enormous sugar-coated, chocolate-dipped, caramel-swirled thank yous to everyone involved.

Firstly, thank you to Kyle for encouraging me to take up this challenge all those months ago and then being so patient with me until the timing was right. To Judith for putting up with me and my endless ramble of thoughts, recipe changes, queries, and requests for ribbons, more pages, and even more pictures. You are an awesome editor and a total joy to work with. To Tara O'Sullivan, Anne Newman, and Jenny Wheatley for being so meticulous with all the fine details that needed double and triple checking. And to everyone else at Kyle Books, who I feel incredibly lucky to work with, because it's a team effort and I am aware that there are more people to thank than space for.

And to the extra-special-double-wonders that are Tara and Tabitha. Words are not enough to thank you both. You completely understood where I wanted to go visually with this book and made it happen—and then made it even better. Days in the studio with the two of you are always the most fun and most creative—even when I ask to do a ridiculous amount of shots in one day, there's sugar and chocolate on

every surface, and the daylight is fading fast. You always create the most beautiful images, all the while laughing and singing along to Madonna! Thank you, wonderful friends. Thank you also to my marshmallow apprentices, Saskia and Liliana; cooking is way more fun when you're involved!

To Lucy Gowans for her incredible design—I love how you have pulled my words and the pictures together so beautifully—

thank you for making this book so special. And to Heather Holden-Brown for coming on board—what's next?

And a special mention to the one and only Mungo, who waits patiently for the cooking to be over so we can get on with the important things in life such as walking miles over the hills to check on the rabbit holes that he has under surveillance. Even though he doesn't care for candies unless they are bone-shaped

and chicken-flavored, he is a vital part of the team.

Finally thank you to Hugh for tasting just about every recipe in every stage of development—it's a tough job but someone's gotta do it. For being so understanding when it felt like my life was being taken over by candies and chocolate and for cooking me the best chile con carne when I needed a spicy respite from sugar. One day I will write a book about pies and kebabs for you. xx